Exploring the World on the Net

Cynthia G. Adams

D1300085

Good Year Books
An Imprint of Addison-Wesley Educational Publishers, Inc.

 Good Year Books

are available for most basic curriculum subjects plus many enrichment areas. For more Good Year Books, contact your local bookseller or educational dealer. For a complete catalog with information about other Good Year Books, please write:

Good Year Books
1900 East Lake Avenue
Glenview, IL 60025

Book design and illustration by Amy O'Brien Krupp.
Copyright © 1999 Good Year Books,
an imprint of Addison-Wesley Educational Publishers Inc.
All Rights Reserved.
Printed in the United States of America.

0-673-57734-1

1 2 3 4 5 6 7 8 9 - ML - 06 05 04 03 02 01 00 99 98

Only portions of this book intended for classroom use may be reproduced without permission in writing from the publisher.

 This Book is Printed on Recycled Paper

Contents

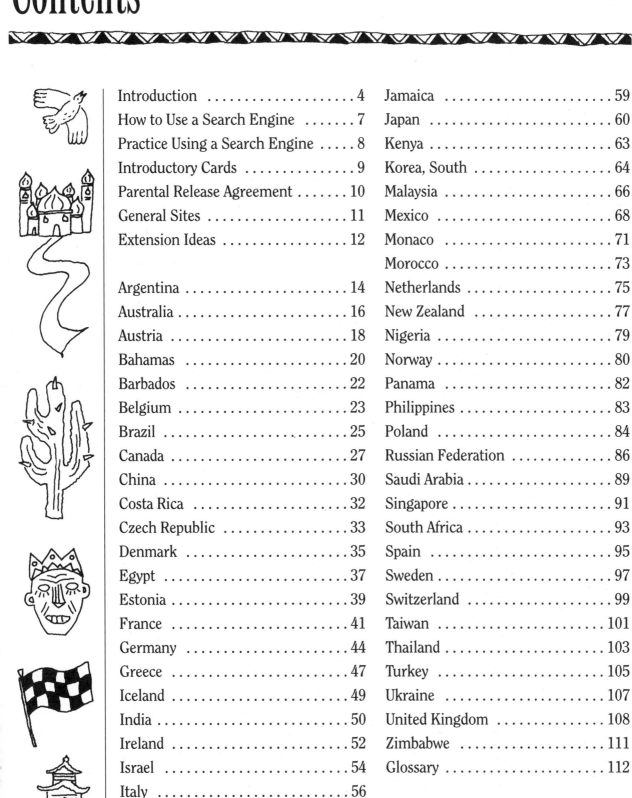

Introduction

Exploring the World on the Net will introduce your students to the cities, landmarks, geography, culture, and history of fifty countries through use of the Internet. Much more than a directory, this book is designed for busy classroom teachers. Each page is divided into two reproducible task cards featuring usable Internet addresses and clear questions, activities, or project suggestions. The tasks encourage critical thinking and geography skills as well as learning. These practical ideas will complement your social studies and multicultural units and provide a valuable resource for individual enrichment or small group learning.

Before using the task cards in this book, familiarize yourself with the terms in the glossary. Once you understand these terms, you will be ready to use the Internet as a tool in your classroom.

Before You Begin

Because the Internet is always changing, it is a good idea for you to check each site before assigning it. You may find that an address has changed or a site has disappeared completely. In some cases, pages may have been moved or renamed. For this reason, many task cards in this book offer two similar addresses so that students' progress will not be slowed.

Check the sites for grade-level appropriateness and to determine a means of evaluating student progress. If you cannot access a Web site, try again at a later time, or you may be able to continue your search by shortening the address from the right. For instance, if **http://www.odci.gov/cia/publications/nsolo/factbook/ca.htm** does not work, try **http://www.odci.gov/cia/publications/**.

After you have determined the best sites for study, your students will be able to search more efficiently if you organize *bookmarks* (or *favorites*) for each content area. Refer to your browser help screen or manual for exact directions on how to accomplish this. You may choose to distribute the list of General Sites on p. 11 and require students to restrict their independent research to those sites.

Your experiences with the Internet in the classroom can be made more positive with careful planning and parent or peer help. They can interpret assignments and help if reading levels are too high. In most cases, all parents should submit a release agreement (p. 10) before students begin to use the Internet.

Copyright © 1999 Good Year Books

How to Use the Cards

The task cards are designed to be duplicated, laminated, cut apart, and placed in your computer center. You may prepare cards for single countries or an entire continent. Students may use the cards during free time, as a structured assignment, or for enrichment according to individual interests and time constraints.

If you prefer, copy the cards and distribute them as consumable materials. Simply check off the specific activities or questions you wish your students to complete. If appropriate, indicate the date by which the assignment must be submitted. Depending on Internet accessibility, the cards may be used for homework assignments. Students may answer on the backs of the cards or on separate sheets of paper. Direct students to sign the completed cards and return them to you for credit. Grade the products according to classroom standards.

You may want to provide a reproducible world map for students to use as they complete the activities on the cards. Several sites provide country maps that students can print and use for tracing routes or labeling landmarks.

As you introduce your students to the Internet using the cards on p. 9, be sure to emphasize that

● every address begins with http://; and
● the site addresses must be entered accurately.

Students should begin by using the addresses on the task cards or from the list of general sites. They can locate additional information by clicking the mouse on the hypertext links within each of these sites.

The bulleted items on the cards are questions that can be answered with information that is readily available in the site. They are primarily reading comprehension or items that give practice in reading and following directions. Items with pencil icons may be critical thinking questions or activity suggestions that will result in a tangible product. They are expanded activities for higher level thinking.

The boldfaced words on the cards match hypertext your students will click on to answer the questions. On the general information card for each country, you will find "search words" to use for independent browsing. Advanced students may use the search words for extended research or if selected sites are no longer available. Use the bookmark or favorites feature of your browser to keep a record of the best Web sites on particular topics.

Using a Search Engine

Search engines provide listings and summaries of addresses on a given topic. You may select a broad category and refine it several times to locate your specific topic. Sometimes it is more efficient to type key words into the bar and push the Enter or Select keys. In most cases, the search engine will list many more sites than you could possibly visit. Take time to read the summaries before making a selection.

Page 7 teaches students how to use search engines. Page 8 provides an activity master for practice in using search engines.

Blocking Software

Software is available to block some of the inappropriate materials on the Internet, although none is fully effective because the Web changes so quickly. Be sure to check with your provider before downloading any of these products.

Cyber Patrol: Allows you to control access to categories of adult material and block words and phrases in chat rooms. Also has a clock that limits online time.
http://www.cyberpatrol.com

Cybersitter: Allows you to block foul language and keeps a list of sites a child has visited.
http://www.solidoak.com

Net Nanny: Comes with a list of blocked sites that is updated monthly. You can add to the list and block access to chat groups and certain words and phrases.
http://www.netnanny.com

Copyright © 1999 Good Year Books

How to Use a Search Engine

You may be asked to use a search engine for additional study. Search engines provide listings and summaries of addresses on a given topic. You may select a broad category and refine it several times to locate your specific topic. To use a search engine, you must:

1. Type and enter the address of the home page for the search engine of your choice. Here are addresses for some common search engines:

> **Yahooligans!** (for kids) . . . . . . http://www.yahooligans.com/
> **Yahoo!** . . . . http://www.yahoo.com/
> **Alta Vista** . . . . http://altavista.digital.com/
> **Excite** . . . . http://www.excite.com/
> **Lycos** . . . . http://www.lycos.com/

2. When the home page appears, type and enter key words that will lead you to the information you need.

For a difficult search, start with a broad topic and gradually make it more specific. For instance, from the Yahoo! home page, you could select Countries, Italy; Travel; or Cities, Rome; then Attractions or Landmarks to find information about the Colosseum, or simply type "Colosseum" into the bar and click the mouse on Select or Enter. Because the Colosseum is a common subject, lots of information will be readily available.

Next you must skim the listings to find the entry(ies) that most nearly fills your needs. Point and click your mouse for access to any Web site in the list.

Practice Using a Search Engine

Search words _____
(teacher fills in)

Search engine(s) used _____

Number of hits _____

Web sites selected _____

_____

Five questions about the topic

1. _____

2. _____

3. _____

4. _____

5. _____

Exchange your questions with a friend.
Answer them using information from the Web sites.

Answers

1. _____

2. _____

3. _____

4. _____

5. _____

Copyright © 1998 Good Year Books

Introductory Card 1
Keypals

Being a keypal is a simple and convenient way to learn about different cultures and create friendships around the world. Some of the sites offer the opportunity to share online activities with classes around the world. After you find and get to know a keypal, the two of you may work together on a school project.

You can use the following sites to select a student (or class) with whom you can exchange e-mail. Most of them ask you to indicate your name, age, and interests, or select from posted lists of students around the world:

Web sites: http://www.reedbooks.com/au/rigby/global/keypal.html

http://www.worldkids.net/clubs/kci/

http://www.mightymedia.com/keypals/

http://www.islandnet.com/~bedford/penpal-k.html

http://www.geocities.com/Heartland/Hills/3415/penpal.html

Introductory Card 2
Cities of the World

Web site: http://www.city.net

You may search any continent, country, or city in the world from this site.

1. From the home page, select the continent.

2. Next select the country, then the city on the clickable maps.

3. When you arrive at the Web site of the city, you will find an index that includes maps, travel and tourism information, city guides, weather, recreation and entertainment suggestions, and photo galleries.

Search the city where you live or a city you have visited, or choose any city you would like to know more about. What would a tourist enjoy about this location? Find an address for a hotel, restaurant, and museum or monument in the city. Describe the city's geographic location within its country and indicate the current weather conditions.

Copyright © 1999 Good Year Books.

Parental Release Agreement

Dear Parent:

We are pleased to announce that Internet access is now available to your child in our classroom. We are excited to be able to provide our students with this valuable learning resource.

Your child will be given assignments to be completed using the Internet. Because the Internet may include some inappropriate material, you may be assured that we will carefully supervise and monitor your child's use.

Students will be given clear guidelines for using the Internet and specific assignments to follow. All students understand that:

● accessing unacceptable materials is strictly forbidden;
● using inappropriate language is strictly forbidden;
● revealing their addresses and phone numbers is forbidden; and
● e-mail is not private.

Please read the above agreement with your child, sign, and return to the teacher by _____ .
　　　　　　　　　　　　(date)

----------------------------------- ✂ Cut along dashed line. -----------------------------------

I have read the terms and conditions for using the Internet.
I realize that a violation will end my access privileges.

Student _____ Date _____

I understand that it is impossible for the school to restrict controversial materials on the Internet. I have discussed appropriate use of the Internet with my child and give my permission for him or her to access the Internet at school.

Parent or Guardian _____ Date _____

Copyright © 1998 Grad Your Books

General Sites

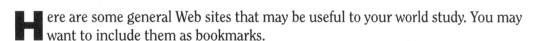

Here are some general Web sites that may be useful to your world study. You may want to include them as bookmarks.

http://www.Yahooligans.com/Around_the_World/People
Home pages of children from various countries.

http://web66.coled.umn.edu/schools.html
Home pages from schools all over the world.

http://www.yahoo.com/Education/K_12/Countries
Home pages from schools all over the world.

http://longwood.cs.ucf.edu/~MidLink/
This magazine, published four times a year, focuses on social and environmental issues around the world.

http://www.nationalgeographic.com/
Students can visit *World Magazine for Kids* online as well as search specific information for science and social studies projects.

http://loki.ur.utk.edu/ut2kids/maps/map.html
http://info.er.usgs.gov
These sites will help your students understand mapmaking. They include satellite images of different parts of the world.

http://www.stolaf.edu/network/iecc
This free service links children with partners in other countries for e-mail keypal projects.

http://www.vtourist.com/vt
Click on an interactive map of the country or city of your choice anywhere in the world.

http://www.odci.gov/cia/publications/95fact/index.html
The CIA provides an index of every country of the world with maps and major facts. These are good for statistics and report information.

http://town.pvt.k12.ca.us/Collaborations/e-school/PCG/postcard.html
This site allows classes from around the world to receive and send postcards. You must register your class for the project and then you will be able to download a list of participating classes.

http://www.cyberkids.com/
This site gives the worldwide youth community an interactive place to express their creativity. View projects by kids and teens all over the world.

http://www.cineworld.com/Main/main_screen.html
Provides an in-depth tour of fifteen great cities of Europe.

Copyright © 1999 Good Year Books.

Extension Ideas

Fine Arts Projects

- Design a travel brochure and poster describing one country.
- Build a model of a landmark in the country.
- Draw a time line depicting a hundred years in the history of one country.
- Research titles of original artwork and musical compositions created by resident artists and musicians.
- Think of at least three ways the country has contributed to the culture of the world (or the region).
- Draw a child in traditional costume.
- Design a postcard from the country. Write about what you've seen and experienced on a trip there.

Writing Activities

- Pretend you are the president or prime minister of the country. Write two laws (or reforms) that would improve life for the people. Considering the needs and strengths of your country, what characteristics would make a good leader?
- Choose a famous landmark in the country. Describe it in detail. How is the landmark significant to the local people?
- Write atlas entries for three different countries.
- Write a diary of a week's vacation in the country.

Social Studies Projects

- Role-play a meeting between two famous people from one country. What is their significance? Pose a current problem for them to resolve.
- Pretend you have just returned from the country. What would you want to tell someone who is planning to visit there?
- Invent two products made from the country's natural resources.
- Sequence a day in the life of a school-aged child. What does he or she study? Describe the school. How is it like and unlike yours?
- What religions are most important in the country? How do religious beliefs affect daily life?
- Look and listen for a current event from the country. Choose an issue, form an opinion, and support your position.

Mapping Activities

- Trace the most direct path from your home to the country. What countries would you pass over?
- Draw a map of the country. Label five major cities or regions.
- Make a topographical or climatological map of the country.

Copyright © 1999 Good Year Books

Task Cards

Copyright © 1999 Good Year Books.

Argentina
General Information

Web site: http://www.lonelyplanet.com.au/dest/sam/argie.htm

- Click on **environment.** Where are Tierra del Fuego and Islas Malvinas? How does Argentina share in their ownership or occupation? What conflict exists in the Islas Malvinas?
- Make an Argentine dictionary showing ten words from the native culture, such as *tango, gaucho, pampas,* and *rhea.*

Web site: http://www.city.net/countries/argentina/

- Click on **World Factbook.** What five countries border Argentina? What direction must you travel from Buenos Aires to reach each border country?
- What products does Argentina export and import?
- Trace the routes of exports and imports to and from Argentina's major trading partners around the world.
- What goods are traded between the United States and Argentina?

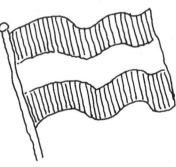

Search words: pampas, Andes Mountains, Cordoba, La Plata, soccer

Argentina
Culture and Language

Web site: http://www.city.net/countries/argentina/

- Click on **culture.** How is European influence reflected in Argentine culture?
- Click on **Spanish for Travelers.** Locate and label all the Spanish-speaking countries in South America. Why is it desirable to be bilingual?
- Click on **numbers.** Practice counting in Spanish.
- Make a bilingual counting chart to share with another class.

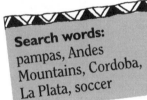

Web site: http://webs.satlink.com/usuarios/t/tarcher/culture.htm

- Click on **compare our cultures** to compare and contrast the activities in the United States and Argentina for one month.
- Take the **culture quiz.**

Web site: http://www.surdelsur.com/indexingles.html

- Click on **cultural identity** and search for information about the tango.
- What **sports** are important to the Argentine culture? How does the location of a country influence the population's choice of athletics?

Copyright © 1999 Good Year Books

Argentina

Geography

Web site: http://www.surdelsur.com/indexingles.html

- Take a **journey into the past** and discover information about the population movement and colonization of the Argentine pampas and Patagonia wilderness.
- What was life like for the people before Argentina became a nation?
- Use the table of contents to go to **Our Land** and click on **geographical regions.**
- ✎ Create a legend and indicate the regions on a map. What kind of work could best be done by the people in each region?

Web site: http://www.lonelyplanet.com.au/dest/sam/argie.htm

- Click on **attractions.** Locate the Iguazu and Parana Rivers on a map of Argentina. List three geographical facts about the Iguazu Falls. What people live in the region? How does the environment affect their culture?
- Click on **off the beaten track.** What would you choose to visit if you had three days of unscheduled time? Explain your choices.

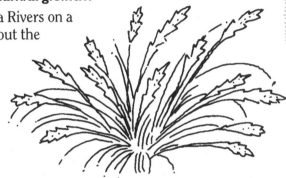

Argentina

Patagonia Wilderness

Web site: http://www.pbs.org/edens/patagonia/histmap.htm

- Click on **Central Steppes.** What is the Petrified Forest? What animals live there?
- Click on **Los Glaciares National Park.** What is Perito Moreno? How is it changing?
- Click on **Ephemeral Lakes.** What is meant by the term *ephemeral lake?* What causes their formation?
- Click on **Peninsula Valdes.** Describe the topography of the peninsula. What wildlife make their home in the area?
- ✎ Show Patagonia on a map of South America. Include a legend to indicate glaciers, deserts, mountains, forests, and water. Make icons for five native wildlife.
- ✎ Fill an imaginary backpack for a virtual trip in the Patagonia wilderness. Write postcards to three of your friends describing your experience.

Copyright © 1999 Good Year Books

Australia

General Information

Web site: http://www.uq.edu.au/~zzgquinn

- What are **Australia's favorite sports?**
- Where will the **2000 Olympics** be held? What factors make this city a good choice?
- Check out the **FAQs.** What is "The Rainbow Serpent"? Send your questions about the "Land Down Under."
- Describe the appearance and behavior of kangaroos. Why do you think they are such fascinating animals? How are they adapted to life in Australia?

Web site: http://www.csu.edu.au/education/australia1.html

- Learn more about **Australia's geography.** What is the highest mountain? longest river? What are the three **landscape features?**
- Compare and contrast geographical features in Australia and the United States on a Venn diagram. Include actual measurements for the highest mountain and longest river.
- Describe a **territory** in detail. How big is it? What is the population? List three interesting facts.
- Write about how a territory would change if a major car manufacturer built a factory there.
- Draw a map of Australia. Label the territories.

Search words:
Australia, Olympics, outback, marsupial

Australia

Travel

Web site: http://tourism.gov.au

- Interested in **traveling to Australia?** Where can you get tourist information? Do you need a visa? What is the best time of year to visit?
- Click on **facts and figures.** How many tourists are expected to visit Australia in the year 2000? From what country do most tourists come?
- Design a T-shirt that might be sold to an Australian tourist.

Web site: http://www.zoo.org.au/hs/hshome.htm

- Visit the **Healesville Wildlife Sanctuary.** Make a list of the native animals and birds you will see.
- Write five interesting facts about the **Tasmanian devil.**
- Make a map of the Healesville Sanctuary. Draw an animal symbol in each section. Include a map legend.

Web site: http://pbr.railpage.org.au/

- Click on **What & Where.** What is **Puffing Billy?** Choose a station. What time does Puffing Billy arrive? How much does a ticket cost?
- What do you imagine you might see as you travel from Belgrave on this steam-powered train?

Australia

Attractions and Landmarks

Web site: **http://www.uq.edu.au/~zzgquinn**

- ● Check out **Australia's attractions and landmarks.** Where could you go scuba diving? climbing? Where could you hear an opera performance?
- ✎ Research the sport of scuba diving. Make a list of necessary equipment. List three other locations popular with scuba divers.
- ✎ How is life different in the Australian Outback than in the cities? Consider daily life, surroundings, and tourism.
- ✎ Research a list of five operas and their composers.

Web site: **http://www.lonelyplanet.com/dest/aust/gbreef.htm**

- ● What is a **coral reef?**
- ● Name five sea **animals** that live on the Great Barrier Reef.
- ● What is the **Crown of Thorns?**
- ✎ Research how coral lives and grows. Where can you see a coral reef in the United States?
- ✎ Make a drawing of one of the sea animals. Label its body parts.
- ✎ How have **people** and **pollution** damaged the reef? What could the government of Australia do to protect it?

Australia

Cities

Web site: **http://www.lonelyplanet.com/dest/aust/act.htm**

- ● How is Canberra different from Sydney and Melbourne?
- ● When is the **Canberra Festival** held?
- ✎ Compare and contrast Canberra, Melbourne, and Sydney on a three-part Venn diagram. Include the population of each city.
- ✎ How is Canberra, Australia, like Washington, D.C.?

Web site: **http://www.lonelyplanet.com/dest/aust/melb.htm**

- ● What **outdoor activities** do the people of Melbourne enjoy?
- ✎ Make a diorama depicting one of the outdoor activities.
- ✎ Work with a group to construct a model of the city centre.

Web site: **http://www.city.net/countries/australia/new_south_wales/sydney**

- ● What are current **weather** conditions in Sydney?
- ● Click on **general information** for a **city guide.** Choose a hotel and restaurant for dinner.
- ✎ If you were visiting Sydney, what would you want to see or do first? Give three reasons to support your choice.

Austria

General Information

Web site: http://www.netwing.at/austria/index_e.html

● What countries border Austria? How does its location make it accessible to large numbers of immigrants? How could such a small country prepare for large numbers of immigrants?

● Click on the **map** of the states of Austria. Select one area, then a village from the list.

✎ Use the enlarged map to locate lodgings in a specific village.

Web site: http://w3.schoenbrunn.at/schoenbrunn/e/tour/homepage.html

● Take a **virtual tour** of the palace and gardens.

✎ Choose five rooms, print the pictures, and explain the purpose of each one. What would life have been like in the palace? What modern conveniences would you miss the most?

✎ Make a drawing of the gardens. What is an *obelisk?*

● What souvenirs are available at the **shop** for the virtual tourist?

✎ Design an order form or a catalog showing five items.

Search words:
Alps, cuisine, Mozart, Austria-Hungary

Austria

Winter Sports

Web site: http://www.anto.com/topski.html

● Check the **snow report** to learn current ski conditions.

✎ What conditions are perfect for skiing and snowboarding? In what countries of the world (other than Austria) do people enjoy these winter sports?

✎ Are there any months when it is impossible to ski in the Austrian Alps?

● Choose a resort from **news for snowboarders and skiers.** Locate its address and e-mail or write for additional information.

✎ What equipment and clothing are necessary for a ski trip? If you have ever gone skiing, what advice would you give a beginner about the sport?

✎ Search the Web for the names of three different Olympic skiing gold medalists.

Austria

Cities

Web site: http://www.anto.com/

- Enjoy a visit to the **Imperial Cities.** Locate the six cities on a map of Austria. How are these cities alike and different?
- What ruling family was important to **Vienna's** history?
- What famous classical musician was born in **Salzburg?** How is the composer memorialized in the city?

Web site: http://www.cineworld.com/Vienna/screen.html

- Enjoy the **sightseeing movie.** Be sure to visit the Opera House and Schoenbrunn Palace.
- ✎ Print your favorite images to use in a visual display. Write a brief description of each landmark. Plot a walking tour on a map.

Web site: http://www.anto.com/faq.html

- Locate the answers to these frequently asked questions: What organization should you contact for travel information? What is the emergency number to contact the police quickly?
- ✎ Trace a travel route between three European capitals and Vienna on a map of Austria. How much time would you need to travel between them by car? by train?

Austria

Culture

Web site: http://www.yahoo.com/Entertainment/Music/Genres/Classical/Composers

- Click on **Classical Period.** Search for the dates of birth and death for these famous Austrian composers: Wolfgang Amadeus Mozart and Franz Schubert.
- ✎ List three compositions by each of them. During what period in music history did these men live?

Web site: http://www.city.net/countries/austria/vienna/

- Click on **Vienna Mozart Concerts**. List three compositions that might appear on a program. Where are the concerts held? What is done to make these concerts more authentic?
- ✎ Listen to one composition and describe the instrumentation.
- ✎ Design an eighteenth-century costume for a man and/or a woman that could be worn to the concert.

Web site: http://eur.com/cuisine/buergerhof/indexe.htm

- What is the **Buergerhof** phone number? Click on **menu** and place your "virtual order"! Include an appetizer, entree, and dessert.
- ✎ Search for and print a recipe for a traditional Austrian dish.

Bahamas

General Information

Web site: http://www.interknowledge.com/bahamas/

- Where are the Bahama Islands located?
- How would you describe the topography and climate of the Bahamas?
- Choose seven **islands.** Read their information and list them in descending order of size and/or population. Circle the islands you've chosen on the map.
- How would life differ between **Freeport/Lucaya** and **West End** on Grand Bahama Island?
- What is unique about the **Inagua** Islands?
- On what island is the capital city, **Nassau,** located?
- What areas of the United States have a climate most similar to the Bahamas? Locate two other tropical island countries on a map of the world.
- How does a tropical climate affect the local economy? How does the climate affect the jobs of local people?

Search words:
Caribbean, islands, marine life, snorkeling, pirates

Bahamas

Travel and Tourism

Web site: http://www.interknowledge.com/bahamas/

- What water sports are popular on the island of **Bimini?**
- Make a list of things children can do in the Bahamas.
- Why do you think so many tourists are drawn to the Bahamas? Interview someone who has visited the Bahamas and share their impressions with the class. Do they plan another visit?
- Contact a travel agency for information about trip planning. Decide on the most economical and direct route to the islands from your hometown. Look at brochures and plan activities for a week's vacation.

Web site: http://www.yahoo.com/Regional/Countries/Bahamas/Travel

- Do you need a passport or a visa to visit the Bahamas?
- Click on **Accommodations and Travel Resources.** List five major hotels or resorts on different islands.
- Click on **Vacation Guide** to find out about special vacations for families. What would be best about a family vacation to the Bahamas?
- What would each member of your family enjoy most about a Bahama vacation?

Bahamas

Ecosystem

Web site: http://www.earthwatch.org/x/Xbalcombw.html

- What species of **dolphins** and **whales** live in the Caribbean?
- Why are scientists attempting to count them and learn about their migratory routes?
- ✎ Read more about dolphins, whales, and seals. Where are their populations concentrated around the world? What are their preferred environments?

Web site: http://www.interknowledge.com/bahamas/

- Click on **Andros Island** and learn more about its barrier reef and marine life. How do Morgan's Cave and the extensive forests complement the ecosystem?
- What is a *chickcharmie?* What is its importance to Andros Island?
- How does the environment on the island of **Inagua** support the production of salt? What unusual animals live on the island?
- ✎ What is a *cay?*
- ✎ Why is it important that the Bahamas preserve their natural beauty? How would life on the islands change if the waters were to become polluted?

Bahamas

History and Culture

Web site: http://www.interknowledge.com/bahamas/bspira01.htm

- Who was **Blackbeard?** What is his significance to the Bahamas?

Web site: http://www.interknowledge.com/bahamas/bshis01.htm

- Trace the migration of the island people who first settled the Bahamas. What is their connection to Spain?

Web site: http://www.interknowledge.com/bahamas/bscal01.htm

- When is Bahamas Independence Day? How is it celebrated?
- What events are offered in the **people-to-people program?**
- ✎ How would you benefit from participation in such a program? Do you believe this is an effective way to learn about another culture?

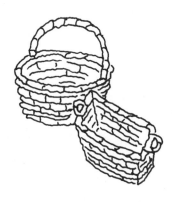

Barbados

General Information

Web site: http://www.barbados.org/btaindex.htm

- Click on **Things to Know** to learn more about the **natural heritage** of the island.
- Where is Barbados located? Name three other islands located nearby.
- ✎ What are the average summer and winter temperatures?

Web site: http://www.tcol.co.uk/barb/barb.htm

- What is this country's most important export? Click on **Macro-Economics** to learn the names of this country's trading partners. What products are imported? Why can't those items be produced locally?
- Click on **Geography** for information about the topography and climate. How are the people and animals affected by the absence of rivers?
- Make a list of flowers and trees that would grow well in Barbados.
- ✎ Make a map showing the topographical information in the article. Include a legend showing the sandy beaches, coral limestone, and rocky areas of the east coast and northeast.
- ✎ Create a map showing average rainfall. Use the **climate chart** to add average temperatures.

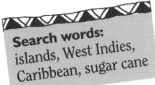
Search words: islands, West Indies, Caribbean, sugar cane

Barbados

Tourism

Web site: http://www.barbados.org/btaindex.htm

- Click on **Things to See.** Use the indexed map or the photo gallery to select and print images of Barbados.
- ✎ What generalizations can you make about the climate and environment of the island from looking at these pictures?
- What are the **seven wonders of Barbados?**
- ✎ Locate them on a map of the island. Plot a route that would allow you to visit each one.
- What **crafts** are made by local people? To whom are these items sold? If you were visiting Barbados, what souvenirs would you want to purchase?
- ✎ Use the information to make a time line and add pictures from your printer. How has life developed and changed since the days of slavery? When did Barbados become an independent nation?
- ✎ What is the status of relations between Barbados and the United States?

Belgium

General Information

Web site: http://www.ib.be/meet/metro.gif

● Study the map for the **Metro Underground.** In what direction and on which lines would you travel from the Centraal Station to Beekant? Roodebeek? Albert?

Web site: http://www.belgium-emb.org/usa/geninfos/geninfos.html

● What are the three constitutionally recognized communities in the **Federal State** of Belgium?

● Click on **Belgium and its Regions.** Draw a map showing the three communities.

✎ What problems would a government and the people need to address when recognizing three national languages?

● Go to **Gastronomy.** What foods are unique to Belgium?

✎ Do research to learn how endive is grown and harvested.

Search words:
Flanders, NATO, chocolate, Walloons, European Union, Luxembourg

Belgium

Cities

Web site: http://www.cineworld.com/Brussels/map_bitmap.html

● Use the **sightseeing movie** to visit the Grand Place in the center of Brussels.

● Click on **museums** for a closer look at works in the **Royal Museum of Fine Arts.** List the paintings that are on display. Visit another museum of your choice.

Web site: http://www.belgium-emb.org/usa

● Pretend you are **Going to Belgium.** Choose **Brugge** from the list of **cities on the net**. Take the **virtual walking tour**. Many people enjoy a boat trip on Brugge's canal system.

✎ How are canals created? Where in the world can a tourist find other extensive canals? How does having a canal system influence the lives of local people?

● Choose several other cities from the list. Look carefully at the architecture. How can you tell if the city is in the French, German, or Flemish section of Belgium?

Belgium

European Union

Web site: http://www.belgium-emb.org/usa/geninfos/geninfos.html
- How does Belgium's geographic location help position it as a world leader? What international organizations are headquartered in Belgium?

Web site: http://www.yahoo.com/Regional/Regions/Europe/European_Union/
- Click on **countries** for a list of those participating in the Union. Mark them on a map of Europe.
- Visit **Law** for a list of **EU basics**. What is the European Union? How did it come into being? How does the Union benefit member nations?
- ✎ Explain how the EU will change travel and trade restrictions among the participating countries.
- ✎ Why do you suppose the European Union is headquartered in Brussels? Give historic and geographic reasons.
- ✎ Use the historical information to create a time line of the EU.

Web site: http://citizens.eu.int/
- Read the **Statistics** in the **News** from the **United Kingdom**.
- ✎ Make a graph showing the numbers of cross-border workers for six EU countries, or indicate how the number of migrant workers has changed between 1990 and 1994.

Belgium

History and Culture

Web sites: http://www.cineworld.com/Brussels/map_bitmap.html
http://www.belgium-emb.org/usa/geninfos/didyknow.html
- What is Manneken Pis? Where is it located?
- Where is Waterloo and why is the location significant in world history?
- What are *tapestries?* Where could you go to see them in Belgium?
- What was the Treaty of Ghent? Where and by whom was it signed?
- Where was the Battle of the Bulge fought?

Web site: http://www.belgian-lace.com/
- Learn about the **History of Belgian Lace** and how it has progressed over time as a cottage industry. What kinds of people are lacemakers?
- ✎ Prepare a report on the four types of Belgian lace. Print the information and explain the uses for each type.

Web site: http://www.giftex.com/belgian/
- What makes Belgian chocolate special? This company will ship **boxed chocolates** anywhere in the world.
- ✎ Choose two different assortments and determine their price in U.S. dollars.

chocolates

Brazil

General Information

Web site: http://darkwing.uoregon.edu/~sergiok/brasil.html

- What is **futebol?** Why is it important to the Brazilian people?
- ✎ Research information about the most famous player, Pele. List five facts about his career.
- Use **information in a nutshell** to learn the names of the capital of Brazil and five major cities.
- What industries are important to the economy of Brazil?
- What natural resources are most available?
- Use **history/customs and courtesies** to find the current **weather conditions** in Brazil.
- ✎ If you were going to visit Brazil this month, what clothes would you pack? Make a chart to show the average temperatures for each month of the year.
- What **national holidays** are the same as or different than those in the United States?
- ✎ Design a greeting card for a traditional Brazilian holiday.

Web site: http://www.embaixada-americana.org.br/holi.htm

- ✎ Design a calendar showing the events and holidays for each month. If you could visit Rio any month of the year, which one would you choose?

Search words:
South America,
soccer, Pele,
rain forest

Brazil

A Virtual Tour

Web site: http://psg.com/~walter/brasil.html

- Enjoy this virtual tour of Brazil with wonderful graphics and lots of links.

- ✎ Choose a **famous person, region of the country,** or **historical event** to search and explain. Prepare a visual display to accompany your report.
- Learn how to make a good cup of **coffee** and why this drink is such a valuable export.
- ✎ Research the health effects of **caffeine.** List five foods (or medicines) that you use which contain caffeine.
- ✎ Poll your classmates to find who drinks coffee regularly, seldom, or never. Graph the results.
- Click on the **map.** Make a set of state flags. Glue them to a large map of Brazil. Label the map with the state name, capital, area, and population.
- ✎ Choose a state to study in depth. Look at the pictures of several cities within that state. Write your impressions.

Brazil

Cities and Landmarks

Web site: http://expedia.msn/com/wg/places/Brazil/RiodeJaneiro/ATACFS.htm

● Click on **Attractions,** then **Historical and Architectural Sights.** Visit two different churches.

✎ Explain how the churches are similar and different on a Venn diagram. How is the architecture like and unlike European cathedrals?

● Visit several museums in Rio de Janeiro. Choose two of your favorites. What is exhibited there? Which museum was built in imitation of the Louvre Museum in Paris, France?

Web site: http://www.geocities.com/The Tropics/3416

● What are the **pluses and minuses** of living in the capital city? Would you want to live there? Explain.

✎ Draw a map of Brasilia. Label the government buildings.

✎ Create your idea of a perfect city. Be sure to consider the environment in your plans.

Brazil

Environment and Tourist Attractions

Web site: http://www.ran.org/ran/kids_action/index.html

● Visit the **tropical rainforest animal** site and learn three ways animals protect themselves in the rain forest environment.

● Click on **Rainforest Action Network** and take a rain forest quiz.

● Discuss the **8 steps that kids can take** to protect the rain forest. Choose three things that you and your classmates can do.

✎ Research a list of rain forest products. Which products are important to your daily life?

✎ Research and debate the pros and cons of beginning a recycling program in your city.

Web site: http://darkwing.uoregon.edu/~sergiok/brasil.html

● Choose one **tourist attraction** to search and explain.

✎ Design a tourist brochure and poster for the attraction.

● Click on **history** and select **customs and courtesies**. If you were a tourist, how would you travel between Brazil's major cities?

● What is a proper greeting for native Brazilians?

✎ What influence has Portugal had on Brazil? Explain.

Canada

General Information

Web site: http://www.tor.ec.gc.ca/text/

● Select an area of Canada and read its weather forecast.

✎ Check conditions in the five regions and create your own weather map.

Web site: http://www.yahooligans.com/Around_the_World/

● Select **Canada** and check the **National Debt Clock.** How much is owed by each man, woman, and child? How does this compare to the **U.S. debt clock?**

● Check out other **Canadian Statistics.** Click on **The Land** for information about the **Geography** and the **Environment.**

✎ What conclusions can you draw from the tables about **forests,** their area, loss due to fires, and efforts at reforestation?

✎ Are Canadians involved in recycling? Support your answer with statistics.

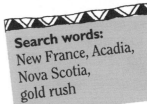

Search words:
New France, Acadia, Nova Scotia, gold rush

Web site: http://parkscanada.pch.gc.ca/parks/main_e.htm

● Click on **SchoolNet** and take the historical trivia quiz.

Canada

Provinces and Territories

Web sites: http://www.alloutdoors.com/allcanada/Province.html

http://www.lib.utexas.esu/Libs/PCL/Map_collection/americas/Canada.GIF

● Make a list of the **provinces and territories.** Outline each area on a map of Canada. Create symbols for the map to indicate the most important natural features.

Web site: http://www-nais.ccm.emr.ca/schoolnet/

● Click on **Our Home** and select a **community** to research. You will find maps to scale and bilingual information prepared by students living there.

✎ Use the **Make a Map** site to create a customized map.

Web site: http://www:yahoo.com/Regional/Countries/Canada/Provinces_and_Territories

● What travel opportunities are available on **Prince Edward Island?** Take a look at the **Island Cam.** What do you see? Images will change every fifteen minutes.

● Read stories of the **Yukon Territory** and the gold rush. Take the **Klondike Quiz** by clicking on **Just for Kids.**

● Search **Newfoundland's Silver Web** for information about local crafts.

✎ Look at several sites in each of the five areas. What crafts are most common? Create a map of Newfoundland and Labrador with appropriate craft symbols and a legend.

Canada

Cities

Web site: http://www.yahoo.com/Regional/Countries/Canada/Cities/

- Search the **city guides** or **events** information for the major cities of **Montreal, Quebec, Ottawa,** and **Toronto.**
- Make a chart of activities in a given week in each city. Trace a route to take you between cities.

Web site: http://www.torontozoo.com

- Visit the **virtual zoo.** Check the **zoo info** and print a **site map.** Answer the riddles for **Kids.** Write a brief report for the featured animals.
- Compare and contrast the Toronto zoo with the zoo located in your town. Why are zoos important to maintaining the world's animal population? How is your zoo helping endangered species?

Web site: http://www.yahooligans.com/Around_the_World/Canada/Maps/

- Click on **Select a Community** and read information prepared by students living there. In which community would you like to live? Support you choice with three reasons.

Canada

Travel and Tourism

Web site: http://www-nais.ccm.emr.ca/schoolnet/

- Click on **Facts About Canada** and take your choice from an extensive listing of geographical facts.
- Use the facts and statistics to create your own Canadian atlas.

Web site: http://www.worldweb.com/ParksCanada-Banff/

- Locate Banff National Park on the map. Search the Web for **visitor information.**
- Write a brief report about the **history** of the park. Print images from the **Photo Gallery** to illustrate your report.

Web site: http://www.quebecweb.com/tourisme/intrjang.html

- Use the **Quebec Tourist Guide** to learn about Canada's French tradition. How does the territory compare to the size of France? Visit **Montreal** for **Tourist Information.**
- How would you get to Montreal from your home? Make a list of attractions that interest you and your family. Choose an accommodation, a museum, and two restaurants. Record the location and average meal price for the restaurants.

Canada

Ecosystem

Web site: http://parkscanada.pch.gc.ca/

- Click on **Natural Science.** What is being done toward **Species Conservation?**
- ✎ Choose one of the species disappearing from the southern areas of Canada to research further.
- Explain Canada's plan for **Land Use Zoning** in the national parks.
- ✎ Make a chart of Canada's endangered species indicating their habitats, features, behaviors, and the reasons they have become endangered. Discuss how human use of the environment has caused problems for plant and animal life.
- What are the eight groups of **Natural Regions** in Canada?
- ✎ Read the information and create a topographical map.
- Return to the **Main Menu.** Click on **School Net Project** and view images of **Parks Canada.**
- ✎ Choose **Classroom Challenges** and take a hidden treasures scavenger hunt.

Canada

History and Heritage

Web site: http://www.cmcc.muse.digital.ca/cmc/cmceng/ca05eng.html

- Visit this site for a tour of **Canada Hall.** Learn about the history of Canada from 1000 to 1890. The high-quality images and text will help you understand the daily life of people in the area. Who were the Acadians?
- Click on **Farming.** What kinds of crops were grown? What livestock was kept? Describe the average farmhouse.
- ✎ Choose a hundred-year period and discuss how life changed during that time for the Canadian settlers.
- ✎ Learn more about the French fur **trade.** What items did they trade? How did the introduction of European tools change life for the natives?

Web site: http://www.schoolnet.ca/ext/aborignal/index.html

- Visit the **First People's Homepage** to learn about the native cultures in Canada. Click on **cultural resources** to find everything from information on **totem poles** to images of **powwow dancing.**

China

General Information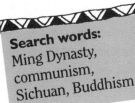

Web site: http://www.freepress.com/yz/beijing/

- ● Check the temperatures on three different **weather reports.** What are the average high and low temperatures?
- ✎ Make a bar graph showing high and low temperatures for any three-month period.

Web site: http://www.chinatoday.com/general/a.htm

- ● China is the third largest country in the world. Which two countries are larger?
- ✎ China has five thousand offshore islands. Locate the South China Sea Islands on a map. How is life on these islands similar to and different from life on mainland China?
- ● What is the relationship of Taiwan to mainland China? When and how did it achieve independence?
- ● Draw the **national flag.** Explain its symbolism.
- ● What is the **population** of China?
- ✎ What is the government doing to discourage overpopulation?
- ● What are the three main **religions** of China?
- ✎ Name the founder and/or diety of each one. Search the net for a picture of Buddha and print it to share with the class.

Search words:
Ming Dynasty, communism, Sichuan, Buddhism

China

Tourism and Travel

Web sites: http://www.freepress.com/yz/beijing/
http://www.city.net/countries/china/beijing

- ● Learn some **travel tips** for China. How would you find a doctor or get medicine if you became ill? Is it safe to drink hotel tap **water?**
- ● What form of **transportation** is most commonly used by Beijingers?
- ● Locate the address and telephone number for one of Beijing's **airlines.**
- ✎ Print a street **map** of Beijing or Tiananmen Square. Plot the most direct route for visiting three important landmarks.

Web site: http://www.cmit.cn.net/province.htm

- ● Travel to **Qinghai** and visit **Bird Island.** What is the area of the island? How many species of birds can visitors see?
- ● What would you see walking down **Barkhon Street** in **Tibet?**
- ✎ Write a diary entry describing the experience.
- ● Visit **the Ruins of Jiaohe** at **Xinjiang.**
- ✎ What generalizations can archaeologists make about ancient civilizations by excavating ruins? How was the city destroyed?

China

Attractions and Landmarks

Web sites: http://www.freepress.com/yz/beijing/
http://www.city.net/countries/china/beijing/essentials/sightseeing.html

● Make a visit to **Tiananmen Square.** Make an aerial map showing several points of interest. What events are held at the Square? Mark the gate to the Forbidden City.

✎ Design a travel brochure with a small map and explanation of each site.

● Visit the **Beijing Attractions.** Make a list of five sites you would most like to visit. Briefly explain the importance of each one to Chinese culture.

Web site: http://www.chinavista.com/beijing/tour.html

● Briefly explain the history of the **Great Wall.** How did the terrain affect work on the Wall?

✎ Write a first-person account of the problems you may have had as a worker on the Wall.

Web site: http://www.chinavista.com/beijing/gugong/!start.html

● Take a virtual tour of the **Forbidden City.** Make a large map of the grounds. Add small drawings of the buildings. Would you have wanted to live in the Forbidden City? Explain.

✎ Who was Pu Yi? What is his importance to the history of China? Why was he forced out of the Forbidden City?

China

Cities and Provinces

Web site: http://www.chinats.com/cshangh.htm

● Where is **Shanghai** located? What is the population?

● List some **interesting places.** Describe Shanghai's climate.

Web site: http://sunsite.au.ac.th/Neighbour/china/regional.html

● Check out **regional cuisine.** What foods do people eat in Beijing and Shanghai? Which foods are grown locally?

✎ How does the typical Chinese diet promote good health and weight control?

Web site: http://www.scsti.ac.cn

● Take a **tour in Sichuan.** What special animals can you see at the city zoo?

✎ Do an in-depth study of pandas. Explain their habitat and food preferences. What efforts are being made to increase their numbers in zoos around the world? Which American zoos have pandas?

Costa Rica

General Information

Web site: **http://webtravel.org/cr/overall-map.html**

● Use the map to identify countries and bodies of water bordering Costa Rica. Between what lines of longitude does Costa Rica lie?

✎ Copy the map and mark the mountains and rivers.

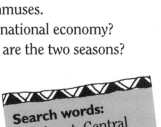

Web site: **http://www.lonelyplanet.com.au/dest/cam/costa.htm**

● Use this site to locate a summary of information about Costa Rica's **culture, economy, geography,** and **natural history.**

✎ What is an *isthmus?* Locate three other countries located on isthmuses.

✎ List three Costa Rican exports. How important is tourism to the national economy?

✎ How does the climate and location affect the tourist trade? What are the two seasons?

Search words:
rain forest, Central America, isthmus

Costa Rica

Travel and Tourism

Web site: **http://www.geocities.com/TheTropics/3425/**

● Read the story of Cocos Island and explain its history. What do people hope to find there?

Web site: **http://www.costanet.com/**

● Click on the **index** for links to **National Parks** and **beaches.** What water sports are available for tourists?

● Use the **information** sites to learn about the topography of the country. What is the general climate?

● Click on **Natural Tour,** then **Ecotours.** Design postcards for the volcanoes and gardens.

Czech Republic
General Information

Web site: http://www.czweb.com/map/czmap.htm

- List the four countries that border the Czech Republic. Give the direction of each one in relation to the Republic.
- Name three rivers in the Czech Republic.
- What are the three largest cities?

Web site: http://www.henge.com/~vspina/czech.html

- Click on **Links** and print a **four-day weather forecast.**
- Click on **History** and answer: What is the connection between the Czechs and Slovaks?
- Why is King Charles IV an **important person** in Czech history?
- Make a drawing of the **Czech Republic's flag.**

Web site: http://www.cesnet.cz/html/cz/basic-information.html

- What **nationalities** live in the Czech Republic? Who is the president of the country?
- Learn to say five **basic travel words** or phrases in Czech by using the Czech/English dictionary.

Search words:
Moravia, Brno, folk music, Prague, Eastern Europe

Czech Republic
Prague

Web site: http://infox.eunet.cz/pis/praha/praha.html

- Visit the locations on **The Royal Mile** and **Old Town Square.**
- ✎ Enlarge the images and print them to use with a sketch map of the areas.

Web site: http://www.open.cz/project/art/cultintr.htm.CP1250

- Take a virtual tour of the **Gallery of the City of Prague.**

Web site: http://www.everydayprague.com/

- You can learn a great deal about life in the Czech Republic by surfing this site.
- ✎ Choose three categories that interest you, read the information, and compare shopping in the Czech Republic and the United States.

Web site: http://www.lonelyplanet.com.au/dest/eur/cze.htm

- ✎ Write a news story explaining what happened on November 17, 1989, in Prague. Who was John Lennon? Click on the icon to see an enlargement of his section of the wall.

Czech Republic

Travel and Tourism

Web site: http://www.lonelyplanet.com.au/dest/eur/cze.htm

✎ Click on **Facts for the Traveller** and determine an average budget for food and lodging. How does it compare to travel in the United States? another European country? Would you say the Czech Republic is a travel bargain? Explain.

● What sports **activities** are available for tourists?

● How would a tourist **get around** the Czech countryside?

Web sites: http://www.brno-city.cz/
http://www.fee.vutbr.cz/BRNO

● Search the **English version** of this site from the Czech Republic's second largest city. Be sure to look at the photos of **historical sites.**

● What are the geographical coordinates of the city?

● As a visitor, what would you find most appealing about the city?

✎ Read about important historical events since the tenth century. Research information about the period of Moravian rule when Brno was the seat of government.

Web site: http://www.castles.org

● Look at an enlarged picture of the **Castle at Prague.**

Czech Republic

Fine Arts

Web sites: http://www.mindsync.com/KUOP/aldbio.htm
http://www.hnh.com/qcomp.htm

● Who was Antonin Dvořák? Where was he born and what were some of his most important compositions?

● Click on **music** and listen to several excerpts.

✎ Briefly define *folk music* and explain how Dvořák used themes of folk music in his work.

✎ Describe the difference between classical and folk music.

Web site: http://www.open.cz/project/art/cultintr.htm.CP1250

● Search the **visual art site** for the names of artists from several periods.

✎ Choose one of the artists to study in depth. What world events (if any) influenced his or her work?

Web site: http://chattanooga.net/~tyman/

● Who is **Mikolas Ales?** In what art medium does he prefer to work?

✎ Explain how Ales's work reflects an interest in nature and pride in his Czech homeland. Make a pen-and-ink drawing that reflects something that makes you proud.

Denmark

General Information

Web site: http://www.lysator.liu.se/nordic/scnfaq33.html

● In this site find an **index** with information about Denmark's **geography, climate,** and **vegetation.** Locate Denmark on a map of the world. What is its capital city?

✎ What is an *archipelago?* Locate another one on a world map. What is a *peninsula?* Locate five others on a world map.

Web site: http://www.bornholminfo.dk/

● Learn about life on the island of **Bornholm** off the mainland of Denmark. What makes the island ideal for a vacation? Describe the location and geology of the island. What are the main industries?

✎ Why is Bornholm a good place for a traveler interested in **nature** and conservation?

Web site: http://www.geocities.com/TheTropics/4597/

● What connection does **Greenland** have with Denmark?

✎ How were Greenland's relations with Denmark affected by World War II?

● Read the information about the **Faroe Islands.** What do you think daily life would be like for children on those islands?

✎ How is life for people on the Faroes improved because of their association with Denmark?

Search words:
Nordic, Scandinavia, Greenland, Faroe Islands

Denmark

Travel and Tourism

Web site: http://www.geocities.com/TheTropics/4597/

● Click on **Tivoli** and compare this famous Danish amusement park with an American one you have visited.

✎ How have amusement parks changed since Tivoli opened in 1843?

Web site: http://www.danbbs.dk/~ais/copenhagen/copgen.html

● Enjoy a picture **Tour of Copenhagen.** What can you learn about the vegetation in the city? Would you say that the Danish people enjoy the outdoors? Explain.

Web site: http://copenhagen.now.dk/

● Pretend you are planning a trip to Copenhagen and will be **Renting a Car.** Choose a car rental agency and record its telephone number.

✎ Search the Internet for a city map of Copenhagen.

Web site: http://www.bornholminfo.dk/

● Locate the address and telephone number of the **Bornholm Welcome Centre.** What assistance might a traveler hope to find there? Describe the environment on the island based on what you see in the photos.

Denmark

History

Web site: http://www.geocities.com/TheTropics/4597/

● How does Denmark honor its **Viking** heritage? What Viking sites can be visited today? Locate them on a map of Denmark.

● During whose rule (and what years) were most of Denmark's **Castles and Manor Houses** built? Which one would you like to stay in? Locate it on a map of Denmark.

● Who is **Queen** of Denmark? Why is she loved by the Danish people? Who are her sons? Where does the royal family live?

Web site: http://viking.no/e/ehome/htm

✎ Prepare a brief report on everyday Viking life. What did they eat? What did they wear? What were their homes like?

Web site: http://www.lysator.liu.se/nordic/scnfaq33.html

● Name the two **Monarchs** who preceded Queen Margrethe II.

● What three additional letters does the **Danish Alphabet** include that the English alphabet does not?

✎ Use the **History** site to explain how Danish society has changed since 1900. Why did Denmark remain neutral in **World War II?**

Denmark

Leisure Time and Sports

Web site: http://www.geocities.com/TheTropics/4597/

● Click on **Danish Pleasures.** Make a list of outdoor activities enjoyed by the Danes. Write three general statements about the environment based on what you know about these sports.

● Click on **What Danes Produce for a Living** and learn what popular children's toy is a Danish creation. Search the Web for more information about these blocks.

Web site: http://www.dif.dk/

● Choose the **English version** of this Olympic site and find out how individual Danish athletes performed. If you prefer, search **Topics to Read** and read a summary of **Team Denmark**'s achievements. How important is **Sport in Denmark?**

✎ Considering the health benefits and social significance of organized sports, what conclusions could you draw about the general well-being of the population? What is meant by the "inherent value" of sports?

Web site: http://www.odkomm.dk/int/hcamuk.htm

● Visit the **Hans Christian Andersen** Museum in Odense. Make a list of his most popular children's books. Where can a visitor see the statue of the Little Mermaid?

Egypt

General Information

Web site: http://city.net/countries/egypt/maps/egypt.html

● Print the **Country Map** of Egypt and connect the parts to make one large map. Use the legend to estimate the distance in miles and kilometers between Cairo and Tel Aviv.

Web site: http://wwwmtv.jrc.it/projects/mercator/gacmap.html

● Locate Egypt on the **Land Cover Map of Africa.** Read the chart and determine what covers most of Egypt. What colors indicate deserts? What part of Africa is covered by deserts?

✎ How does living in the desert influence the lives of the Egyptian people?

Web site: http://www.wtgonline.com/country/eg/cc.html

● Study the climate charts for Cairo. In what months did the least rain fall?

✎ How do you think Egyptians tolerate the lack of rainfall? How would the lack of rainfall affect agriculture?

✎ Make a bar graph showing the hours of sunshine each month.

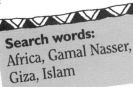

Search words:
Africa, Gamal Nasser, Giza, Islam

Egypt

Mummies, Pyramids, and Hieroglyphics

Web site: http://guardians.net/egypt

● Select Mummies from the contents list. This site has links to information about mummies.

Web site: http://www.pbs.org/wgbh/pages/nova/pyramid/

● What is the **Sphinx?**

● Learn about the **History of Giza** and the pyramid builders.

✎ Make a diagram of your path after you **Enter.**

● Click on **Excavation** to be part of a recent **Dig.** What are archaeologists learning about ancient civilizations?

Web site: http://www.iut.univ-paris8.fr/~rosmord/PortraitE.html

✎ Follow the directions for **Your Name in Hieroglyphics** and send an e-mail to see your name written in the ancient Egyptian form.

Web site: http://www.iut.univ-paris8.fr/~rosmord/AlbumE.html

● Choose the **Album in English.** What do the carvings and artwork tell you about the ancient Egyptians?

Egypt

Nile River and Aswan High Dam

Web site: http://www.arab.net/egypt/geography/et_nile.html

- Click **Geography** to discover the mineral resources of Egypt. You may do a search of this site by typing in concepts or key words.
- Read about the Nile River. Look at a map showing Egyptian cities. How has the Nile Valley influenced the settlement of people?

Web site: http://website1.lanminds.com/Odyssey/wk1Nile.html

- How long is the Nile River? What is unusual about its flow?
- Why is the mouth of the Nile called a delta?

Web site: http://lcweb2.loc.gov/cgi-bin/query/D?cs:5:./temp/~frd_QQhC::

- Read about how agriculture has improved since the building of the **Aswan High Dam** in 1964. What is the difference between basin and perennial irrigation?
- ✎ How has the dam affected Egypt's economy and the quality of life of its people?

Egypt

Travel and Tourism

Web site: http://egyptcenter.com/

- Click on **Pictorials,** then **Photos of Egypt** and view **Photos of Cairo** or look at the **ten best photos** of the country.
- The **General Travel** site has the **Travel Channel's Spotlight on Egypt.** The **Information Guide** will help with phrases in Arabic as well as tips for assuring a good visit.
- Click on **Culture** and enjoy a visit to a **Virtual Museum.** Describe what you like (or dislike) about Egyptian art.

Web site: http://www.coptic.net/Egypt/Cairo/

- How would you travel to reach Cairo, Egypt, from your home? Trace the most direct route. What modes of transportation would you choose?
- By what other names is Cairo called?
- Check the **Visitor Guide** for information about where to stay, what to eat, and things to see.
- ✎ Choose an area on the clickable **Map** to enlarge. Plan a walking tour indicating the sites and their compass directions.
- Click on **Other Cairos Around the World.** There are seven in the United States. Locate them on a U.S. map.

Estonia

General Information

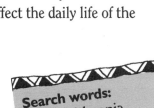

Web site: http://www.ibs.ee/history/index.html

● On what date did Estonia become an independent nation-state?

● What other nations occupied Estonia during its long history?

Web site: http://www.wtgonline.com/info.html

● Click on **E,** and select **Estonia** from the list of countries.

✎ Locate all three Baltic States on a map of the world. Mark Estonia's capital city.

● Go to the **Climate Chart Page** and review the average temperatures for each month. Why do you suppose Estonia has so few hours of daily sunshine between October and February?

✎ Describe how living without much sunshine for those months would affect the daily life of the Estonians.

Web site: http://www.city.net/countries/estonia/maps/

● Enlarge the **map.** What lines of longitude does Estonia lie between? What lake borders Russia and Estonia?

● About how far is it in kilometers from Tallinn, Estonia to Riga, Latvia? from Tallinn to St. Petersburg, Russia? How would you travel to each of these destinations?

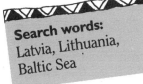

Search words:
Latvia, Lithuania, Baltic Sea

Estonia

Nature and the Environment

Web site: http://www.ciesin.ee/ESTCG/NATURE/

● Use the information to make a map of the **geological** and **mineral resources** in Estonia.

✎ How are new islands being formed along the coast?

✎ How has the land been altered by glaciers?

● Click on **Environmental Protection and Information.**

✎ What pollution problems is Estonia facing? In what part of the country is pollution the most serious? Why is it difficult to enforce water and air quality standards? What should the government do to improve the environment of Estonia?

Web site: http://www.zzz.ee/zoo/pildid/

● Check out **Pictures of Animals** and **Events** at the Tallinn zoo. View the **Mosaic of Animals.** Enlarge your favorite animal and print its picture.

✎ Do additional research and report on the animal you've chosen. Determine its natural habitat and country of origin. Is it endangered? If so, what is being done to preserve the species?

Estonia

Hiiumaa, Saaremaa, and Muhu Islands

Web site: http://www.city.net/countries/estonia/hiiumaa_island/
- Enlarge the map to see the exact location of the islands.
- Click on **Top Ten Questions** and find out how to get to Hiiumaa Island. How large is the island? How many people live there? What can a tourist expect to do on the island?

Web site: http://www.waldec.tt.ee/saaremaa/
- Read the **Nature** of Saaremaa to learn how the island was formed. What wildlife species make their homes on the island? How does wildlife on the mainland differ from that on the island?
- How do you think the animals and birds got to Saaremaa? Create a sketch map to explain their migrations.

Web site: http://www.interlog.com/~muhu/php.cgi/~muhu/history.html
- Look closely at artifacts uncovered by archaeologists working on Muhu island. Visit Muhu St. Catherine's Church and windmills once used by every household.
- How would you describe life on the island? Would this be a good tourist destination? Explain. Design a travel poster for Muhu Island.

Estonia

Government

Web site: http://www.ciesin.ee/ESTONIA/map.html
- Click on the **Flag of Estonia.** Explain the symbolism of the colors.
- Click on the **Coat of Arms.** Explain the symbolism of the items pictured on the coat of arms.

Web site: http://www.ciesinee/ESTCG/
- Read information in the **State and Political System** sites. Who is Estonia's **Prime Minister?**
- Visit the office of the president and **Meet the First Family.**
- Click on **What's New** and read recent government **Press Releases.**
- Where has the Estonian president traveled in the past six months? With whom has he visited? As you skim the articles, decide what the most serious matters concerning Estonia's security and economy appear to be.

France

General Information

Web site: http://www.city.net/countries/france/

● Enlarge and center the **Map** of France. What countries border France on the east? How would you describe the western border?

● Click on **1996 World Fact Book France.** What are the geographic coordinates for France? Locate the French territories on a map of the world.

✎ What is **Corsica**'s connection to France?

✎ Make a graph based on the temperatures listed at the right of the home page.

Web site: http://www.city.net/countries/france/

● Choose a **region** of France. Locate it on the map and check the **travel and tourism** information. Identify three **cities** within the region.

✎ Write a short paragraph about why this region would or would not make a good vacation destination.

Web site: http://www.wtgonline.com/country/fr/gen.html

Search words:
French Riviera,
Normandy, Versailles,
chateaux

● What is the general **climate** of France? Look at the **Climate Chart Page** and write five questions about temperature that could be answered by a classmate.

France

World War II

Web site: http://www.historyplace.com/worldwar2/

● Click on the **Timeline** to see news photos of the occupation and liberation of Paris during World War II.

✎ How did the Nazi occupation affect the daily life of Parisians?

✎ Write a headline and news article about the day the Germans left Paris.

Web site: http://www.grolier.com/wwii/wwii_degaulle.html

● Read this biography of **Charles de Gaulle**.

✎ Create a time line showing de Gaulle's career as a leader of the French Resistance, through the Fifth Republic and the Algerian War, to his resignation in 1969.

✎ Design a monument and write an epitaph to Charles de Gaulle.

France

Paris, City of Lights

Web site: http://www.paris.org/

- From this site you can tour **The City.** Select **Scenes from Paris** to view. Analyze the pictures for information about traffic and people.
- Click on **Paris Culture (Monuments)** and read about the Eiffel Tower, Notre Dame, and the Arc de Triomphe.
- What is the Champs Elysees? What is its significance to the French people?
- Send an **e-mail** to the Paris pages. You will be answered in seven to ten days.
- Make a diagram of the Eiffel Tower labeling what tourists can see from each of the three platforms.

Web site: http://www.cineworld.com/Main/main_screen.html

- Choose **Paris.** Explore the clickable **Map Guide to Sights.** Select and view the enlarged sights. Write a paragraph explaining the location of each one.
- Select an area of Paris and print the **Walking Tour** map. Trace the path of a walk that will take you past at least two monuments. Write the directions.
- If possible, view the **Sightseeing Movie.** Use what you know to explain why Paris is a popular tourist destination.

France

Chateaux of the Loire Valley

Web sites: http://people.mne.net:1234/7217/LOIRE.HTM

http://www.tripod.com/bin/travel/browser/europe/08FRANCE_8/
The_Loire_Valley/

- Use these sites to find details about the cities of **Blois, Angers, Orleans,** and **Tours,** as well as directions on how to get there and **Where to Sleep and Eat.** What sites are **Near Tours**? How do people travel in this area?

Web site: http://www.maison-de-la-france.com:8000/ouest/ukloire.html

- Go to the index and click on **Chateaux (English).** This site gives you a summary and small images of several chateaux of the Loire Valley. Mark their locations along the Loire River.

Web site: http://www.touraine.com/tourisme/loire-valley.html

- Tours is the city at the heart of the Loire Valley. Use the online service to select a driver–tour guide and hotel. How are these services and accommodations unique to France?
- Estimate the distances between Paris and Tours, Angers, Orleans, and Blois. What would be the best way to travel to each of these cities?

France
Cuisine

Web site: http://www.epicuria.fr/

✎ Choose twelve food words from the French language. Make a chart showing a picture of each food with its name in English and French.

✎ Search the Internet for a **recipe** for a French food that you believe you would enjoy. Prepare enough to share with the class.

Web site: http://www.interfrance.com/en/fc/ga_la-cuisine.html

✎ Use the information to create a menu for a dinner in France. Be sure to include an appetizer, entree, and dessert.

France
Art and Music

Web site: http://www.paris.org/Musees/

● Choose the **Musee du Louvre** from the list of museums and proceed through the floor plan to a specific kind of artwork that interests you.

✎ Select a painting or statue from the **Collections** at the Louvre. Research its background and the biography of the artist.

Web site:
http://citywww.lacc.cc.ca.us/BUSINESS/csit137/impres.htm

● At the **WebMuseum, Paris,** you can learn about the Impressionist movement in art. Look at the works of several famous painters and think about how social change affected the movement.

Web site: http://www.fire.summary.net/debussy/home.html

● Enjoy a concert of Impressionist music while viewing famous paintings done by masters of the period. Click on the paintings for more information.

✎ Search the Internet for additional information about Claude Debussy and Maurice Ravel. Name three compositions by each composer.

Mona Lisa

Germany

General Information

Web site: http://www.chemie.fu-berlin.de/adressen/brd-fact.html

- What European countries border Germany? Indicate the compass direction of each one. What bodies of water border Germany?
- What are Germany's natural resources?
- ✎ Make a graph to show the percentage of German males and females who are 0–14 years old, 15–64 years old, and 65 years old and over.

Web site: http://www.wtgonline.com/country/de/gen.html

- Read the **climate charts** and determine which months had the greatest rainfall in Berlin and Frankfurt.

Web site: http://www.lib.utexas.edu/Libs/PCL/Map_collection/europe/Germany.jpg

- Use the key to estimate the number of miles between Berlin and Hamburg and then Frankfurt and Heidelberg on the Autobahn.
- ✎ Locate the Rhine River Valley, Black Forest, and Bavaria in western Germany. How would you describe the environment of these areas? Mark the Alps and include these major cities on your map: Munich, Stuttgart, Bonn, Berlin, Cologne, Leipzig, and Frankfurt.

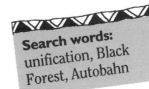

Search words:
unification, Black Forest, Autobahn

Germany

Berlin

Web site: http://www.berlin-info.de/english/sights/stadt.html

- **Choose a Sight** on the city map. Would you say that Berliners enjoy and appreciate the outdoors? Label five sites on a city map. In what area are most of the museums and churches located?

Web site: http://www.cineworld.com/Main/main_screen.html

- Choose **Berlin** and take the **Sightseeing Tour.** Click on the map and find information about the Palace at Potsdam and Ka De Wa, the largest department store in Europe.
- Click on **Museums.** Where can a Berliner see art treasures from Egypt? Greece and Rome?
- ✎ What is a *frieze?* Describe the valuable frieze on display at the Pergamon Museum.

Web site: http://www.berlin-info.de/index_e.html

- Click on **sightseeing tour** and enjoy the city. Which sites were erected before and after the war? How do they differ?
- Enlarge the photo of **Potsdamer Platz.** Why is this now a major construction site? What is the significance of Potsdamer Platz to the German people?

Germany
Unification

Web site: http://www.chemie.fu-berlin.de/BIW/wall.html

● Read this site for background information and details about the Berlin Wall. On what date were citizens of West Berlin first forbidden to go to the east? When was the border reopened? What stands on the site of the wall today?

✎ How has the German economy changed because of unification? What changes must be made in East German manufacturing methods? Why are these changes necessary?

Web site: http://www.chemie.fu-berlin.de/bilder/mauer.gif

● View this large photograph of the Brandenburg Gate dividing East and West Berlin. What feelings were these people probably experiencing as the wall fell? How did the fall of the wall affect families who had been living in a divided Berlin?

Germany
Castles

Web sites: http://germanworld.com/castles.htm
http://www.allgaeu-schwaben.com/cneuschwanstein.html

● What is unusual about **Castle Neuschwanstein?** Who was Richard Wagner? What was his relationship with King Ludwig II?

● Click on **Castle Linderhof** and visit another of Germany's famous castles.

✎ Compare and contrast the two castles of Ludwig II on a Venn diagram.

Web site: http://www.abest.com/~phontics/castles.htm

● This site has beautiful photos of six castles near Heidelburg.

Web site: http://www.allgaeu-schwaben.com/castle.html

● Search the list of Bavarian castles by **name** and locate them on the **map.**

✎ How might these castles affect the economy of the area? What jobs would be created because of tourists visiting the castles?

Germany

Travel and Tourism

Web site: http://www.lonelyplanet.com.au/dest/eur/ger.htm

● Click on **events.** What German festivals are fun for tourists?

● What is the average price of a dinner and hotel room in Germany? What can a tourist do to save **money?**

✎ Read about the Frisian Islands in **Off the Beaten Track.** Locate the islands on a map. Measure their distance from two major German cities. Why would the islands be a good tourist destination?

Web site: http://server2.powernet.net/~hflippo/german/vwfotos.html

● This site has a large group of wonderful pictures of German life. All the pictures have a brief explanation and can be enlarged. (Most of the photos are of Germany, though some picture Austria and Switzerland.)

✎ How is driving on the German Autobahn different from driving on a U.S. highway?

● Be sure to enlarge pictures of the **The Wall.**

● What is the **East Side Gallery?** Why is it a problem?

✎ Explain how movement was restricted because of the Berlin Wall.

Germany

Famous People

Web site: http://www.nobel.se/laureates/physics-1921-1-bio.html

● Read the brief biography of **Albert Einstein.** For what work did he receive the **Nobel Prize?**

Web site: http://www.altusdesign.com/beethoven

● Read biographical information about the composer and check the **Timeline of Beethoven's Life,** which has illustrations of Beethoven over the years. The time line also makes connections to other world historical events.

✎ Choose a famous German (past or present). Research events in his or her life and create a time line that also includes connections to world history.

Web site: http://www.rivertext.com/busch.shtml

● Read a brief biography of **Wilhelm Busch,** painter, cartoonist, and poet, and enjoy his cartoons, **Max & Moritz** and **The Mole.**

✎ After reading his work, explain why Busch is called the "father of the modern comic strip." Illustrate one of his poems and rewrite it in your own words.

Greece

General Information

Web site: http://www.greekembassy.org/

- Click on **general information** to learn about the **geography** of Greece. What **flora** and **fauna** are native to Greece?
- Describe the general **topography** of Greece. What percentage of the land is hilly and mountainous? What percentage is cultivated?
- What are Greece's **natural resources?**

Web site: http://www.ntua.gr/weather/

- What are the current weather conditions in Athens? Check the four-day forecast and use a calculator to compute the temperatures in degrees farenheit ($F = c \times 1.8 + 32$).

Web site: http://agn.hol.gr/hellas/map.htm

- You can zoom on any Greek location from this map. Use it to learn more about the Greek islands, particularly **Crete.**
- ✎ How would you compare the quality and pace of life on Crete with that of Greece? Give details to support your position.

Search words:
Parthenon,
mythology, Olympia,
Attica, Crete

Greece

Athens and the Acropolis

**Web sites: http://www.vacation.forthnet.gr/athens.html
http://www.vacation.forthnet.gr/athmap.gif**

- What sights can a visitor see near the Acropolis?
- Use this map to plan a walk from your hotel to the Parthenon. Print the map and make a mark (anywhere) to indicate the location of your hotel. Trace the most direct route to the Parthenon.
- ✎ Explain the directions in words to a classmate.

Web site: http://www.culture.gr/2/21/211/21101m/e211am01.html

- Take a **tour** of the Acropolis museum.
- Choose three exhibited items to explain in your own words. What are the Caryatids?
- ✎ Search the Internet for information about the Parthenon Marbles.

Greece

Architecture

Web site: **http://chs-web.neb.net/usr/katelevy/greek/greek.html**

● At this site read about the **history** and characteristics of classic Greek architecture. What are the three basic orders?

✎ Build or draw examples of Doric and Ionic columns.

Web site: **http://www.thais.it/architettura/greca/schede/ sc_00046_uk.htm**

● Click on **Alphabetical Index of the Places.** You can enlarge photos of **Olympia** and **the Acropolis** as well as several other interesting sites.

✎ What do you think it would be like working as an archaeologist at one of these locations? What might you hope to find?

Greece

Ancient Olympic Games

Web site: **http://www.culture.gr/2/21/211/21107a/e211ga02.html**

● Read information about Olympia, the birthplace of the Olympic Games and an area of archaeological significance. What artifacts from Olympia are exhibited at the Louvre Museum in Paris?

✎ Who was Zeus? What is his connection to the Olympic Games and Olympia?

Web sites: **http://www.culture.gr/2/21/211/21107a/og/games.html**
http://www.culture.gr/2/21/211/21107a/og/events.html

● Who was the founder of the ancient Olympic Games?

● What was the "sacred truce"?

✎ Make a booklet with illustrations and definitions of the ten events that were part of the Olympic Games in the fifth century.

Iceland

General Information

Web site: http://www.lysator.liu.se/nordic/scnfaq51.html
- How was the island of Iceland formed?
- What is unusual about the way Icelanders heat their homes?

Web site: http://islandia.nomius.com/people/
- Click on **Name System** and learn about the way Icelanders name their children. What would your name be under this system?
- What **Sports** are popular in Iceland? Why are handball and chess favorites?

Search words:
volcanic islands, hot springs, geothermal power, glaciers, Leif Eriksson

Web site: http://www.nyherji.is/~gunnsi/mapa.htm
- What kinds of things appear on Iceland's **stamps?**
- Design a glacier or volcano stamp.

Web site: http://vulcan.wr.usgs.gov/Volcanoes/Iceland/framework.html
- Look at these interesting images of a volcanic eruption under Vatnajokull, Iceland. How would the surrounding areas be affected by the eruption?
- How do volcanoes form islands?

Iceland

Travel and Tourism

Web site: http://islandia.nomius.com/
- Click on **Tourist Information** for several links related to travel. If you have a question about Iceland, send an **e-mail** to a tourist board listed under **Useful Addresses.**

Web site: http://www.btinternet.com/~kevram/icehome.html
- What is Iceland's **Blue Lagoon?** Read the text and look at the photos.
- Where else in the world can you find geothermal springs?
- Click on **Geyser.** Read the text and look at the photos.
- What causes a geyser to erupt? In what U.S. national park can you see a geyser?

Web site: http://www.nyherji.is/~gunnsi/mapa.htm
- How would you describe the environments of **Austfiror** and **Isafjorour,** the eastern- and northernmost points on the map?
- How do those locations compare to **Reykjavik,** Iceland's capital city? How is Reykjavik similar to or different from other Scandinavian capitals (Oslo, Norway; Copenhagen, Denmark; or Stockholm, Sweden)?

India

General Information

Web site: http://www.indiagov.org/

● How many **states** are there in India? Click on two states and compare and contrast their environments, cities, monuments, and people. Which part of India has the greatest natural beauty? Which has the densest population? Which would have the greatest appeal to tourists?

Web site: http://www.city.net/countries/india/

● Click on **World Fact Book.** Make a map showing the **terrain** of India. Include the Ganges River and mark the locations of bordering countries.

✎ Make a temperature chart using weather information on the opening screen.

Web site: http://www.tiac.net/users/whb/India.html

● Enjoy the images on this **Virtual Tour** of India. Look at several photos. Describe the environment and use the pictures to draw conclusions about the geography and climate of India.

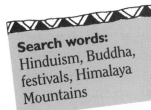

Search words:
Hinduism, Buddha, festivals, Himalaya Mountains

India

Culture

Web site: http://www.indiagov.org/culture/overview.htm

● Click on **Monuments** and visit the Taj Mahal. Where is the monument located? For whom and for what purpose was it built?

● Look at the other Indian monuments. What characteristics do they have in common?

● Click on **Musical Instruments.** Make a list of instruments sorted by type.

✎ If possible, listen to a recording of Indian music played on authentic instruments. Describe the sound. How is it different from western music?

● What foods are common in Indian **Cuisine?** How are they prepared?

✎ Search the Internet for Indian recipes and plan a simple meal.

Web site: http://www.incore.com/india/commun.festival.html

● Use these sites to find information about India's many **festivals.** It is said that India has a festival for every day of the year. Why do you think this is so?

✎ Choose **Holi** or **Diwali.** Explain the history and customs of the celebration.

India

Old and New Delhi

Web site: http://www.lonelyplanet.com.au/dest/ind/del.htm
- Click on **Photo Gallery of New and Old Delhi** to see black and white pictures of daily life in the city. The **Slide Show** has colored photos of landmarks and shopping.
- What is sold in the open-air markets of Delhi?

Web site: http://www.hotwired.com/rough/india/delhi/city.html
- Click on **Old, New, and South Delhi** for information about the sites available in each part of the city.
- Draw a map that shows the sections of the city. Make a picture key for your map to help identify the landmarks.

Web site: http://www.hotwired.com/rough/india/delhi/basics.html
- Click on the **Festivals of Delhi** and make a calendar of events for the next two months. Draw a postcard for one of the upcoming festivals.

India

Travel and Tourism

Web site: http://www.lonelyplanet.com.au/dest/ind/ind.htm
- Click on **Rajasthan** on the map. Read about the tribal customs that make these people different from other Indians.
- Select the capital city, **Jaipur,** on the clickable map and look carefully at the photos. What is unusual about the buildings in Jaipur?
- Click on the **Ganges** and **Northern India** to see beautiful photos of the Taj Mahal. Varanasi is the religious capital of India. Why do Hindus gather on the banks of the Ganges?
- Research the beliefs and practices of the Hindu religion. Give three examples of how Hinduism influences daily life in India.

Web site: http://www.fodors.com/stt.cgi?dest=Delhi@23
- How long does it take to fly to Delhi from New York? Los Angeles? Chicago?
- What health risks must a traveler consider? Why is this an important concern considering the climate of India?
- What customs must a tourist observe when visiting a religious monument? private homes?

Ireland

General Information

Web site: http://www.iol.ie/~discover/welcome.htm

- Click on **Facts** to learn basic information about Ireland. What is the current population? What is the capital city?
- Select the **Presidential Web Site** and take a **tour** of the state house. Who is the current **President of Ireland?**
- Enjoy the photographs in **Images of Ireland** and the **Lighthouse** sites. How would you describe the Irish coastline?

Web site: http://www.wtgonline.com/info.html

- Click on **I** and select **Ireland.** Look at the map of Ireland. What bodies of water border the country? Give the compass direction for each one.

Web site: http://www.interknowledge.com/northern-ireland/index.html

- Visit the **main attractions** of Northern Ireland (part of the United Kingdom) from this page.
- ✎ How does life differ in the north? How do the people spend their time? make a living?

Search words:
Irish Step Dancing, Cork, leprechaun, Belfast

Ireland

Myths and Legends

Web site: http:cpl.lib.uic.edu/003cpl/stpatricksmisc.html

- Use these sites for factual information about St. Patrick and the celebration of his holiday.
- What are the **three myths** associated with St. Patrick?

Web site: http://www.jex.com/patty/

- Read the **Traditional Irish Blessing,** then click on **Everything Irish** to answer **What is a Leprechaun?**

Web sites: http://www.blarney-stone.com/brice.html
http://www.aardvark.ie/cork/blarney.html

- Read the legend of the **Blarney Stone.** What is "the gift of eloquence"?
- Enlarge the pictures of **Blarney Castle.** What was the original use for the stone? Locate the castle (in County Cork) on a map of Ireland. About how far is it from Dublin?

Ireland

Dublin

Web sites: http://www.visit.ie/hpg_dbln.htm
http://www.city.net/countries/ireland/dublin/maps/

- Click on **Visit Dublin.** From the list of Dublin's **Top Attractions,** choose five to locate on a city map.
- Use the **Quick Visit Guide** to select an accommodation and place to eat. Locate them on the city map.

Web site: http://www.city.net/countries/ireland/dublin/essentials/factsheet.html

- Calculate the average **temperatures** for each month and design a bar graph showing the information.

Web site: http://www.travelchannel.com/spot/ireland/welcome.htm

- Click on **Travel Essentials** and explain how you would get to Dublin. Name the two airports. How would you travel to Ireland from England, Scotland, Wales, or France?
- Locate the ferry ports in Dublin and County Cork.

Ireland

Art and Music

Web site: http://www.geocities.com/SouthBeach/Marina/4870/music.html

- To hear traditional Irish tunes, click on **Celtic Midi Files.**
- What instruments are commonly used in Irish folk music? Research the lyrics to some of the songs. What common themes run through the music?

Web site: http://www.iol.ie/~scooney/tradsite.html

- You can find music and lyrics to many traditional Irish favorites in the **Irish and Swedish Tunebook.**
- Choose one of the tunes to play on a recorder or piano.

Web site: http://www.synergy.ie/crawford/

- Visit the Crawford Art Gallery in County Cork. You can enlarge several of the paintings. Read the text provided for insight into the work of Irish artists.

Israel

General Information

Web site: http://www.odci.gov/cia/publications/nsolo/factbook/is.htm

● What are the geographic coordinates of Israel? What countries border Israel?

✎ Make a map showing the terrain of Israel with its highest and lowest points.

● When is Israeli Independence Day? Draw the Israeli flag.

Web site: http://www.macom.co.il/hebrew/index.html

● Click on **Hebrew Alphabet** to see and hear the letters. You can also hear **Numbers and Counting** and **Useful Words** for tourists.

Web site: http://www.cnts.ab.ca/nt_inf.htm

● What countries are represented in the Jewish communities of Israel?

● What are the three main religions of Israel?

✎ How does this diversity benefit or harm Israel? Check current events for up-to-date information.

Search words:
Golan Heights, Gaza Strip, West Bank, kibbutz, Haifa

Israel

Kibbutzim

Web site: http://www.yahoo.com/Regional/Countries/Israel/Kibbutzim/

● What is a *kibbutz?* Choose at least five of the kibbutzim from the menu. Locate each of them on a map of Israel and make a small picture to indicate their products or business.

Web site: http://www.gilboa.co.il/kibbutz.htm

● Read the **Story of Beit Hashita**, a successful kibbutz in the Jezreel Valley. What does life on a kibbutz provide its members? What are they expected to do as part of the community?

● Click on **Tourism** to understand how the kibbutz accepts visitors.

● What **Cottage Industries** are important to Beit Hashita?

✎ Make a chart comparing life in a kibbutz with life in a small U.S. city. Do you think the cooperative concepts of kibbutz life would be successful in America? Explain.

Israel

Tourism

Web site: http://www.inisrael.com/tour/dead/dead.htm

● Click on **General Information** and **Map.** Describe the climate of the Dead Sea area. What archaeological sites are near the Dead Sea?

✎ Look at Dead Sea Scroll fragments or enlarge any of the pictures on the home page. Why are the Dead Sea Scrolls important?

● What is unusual about the waters of the Dead Sea?

Web site: http://travel.yahoo.com/destinations/Middle_East/countries/Israel

● Click on **Attractions.** How is the Old City of Jerusalem divided? What is the Western Wall? Via Dolorosa?

● What two destinations are most popular with religious pilgrims?

✎ Describe how Tel Aviv is different from Jerusalem.

✎ Search the Internet for more information about Masada, a fortress near the Dead Sea.

Israel

Jerusalem and Tel Aviv

Web site: http://jeru.huji.ac.il/jerusalem.html

● This site has photos and information about **The Old City, New City**, and **Jerusalem Gates.** How would you describe the terrain of Jerusalem from these pictures?

Web site: http://www.israel-mfa.gov.il/mfa/capital/jlemmain.html

● At this site you can visit the **City of David, The Temple Mount,** and the **Western (Wailing) Wall**.

Web site: http://www.lib.utexas.edu/Libs/PCL/Map_collection/world_cities/TelAviv.jpg

● Print the street map of Tel Aviv.

Web sites: http://www.agmonet.co.il/list/li04011.htm
                http://www.agmonet.co.il/list/li04015.htm
                http://www.agmonet.co.il/list/li04055.htm

● Locate three of the museums on the street map of Tel Aviv.

● Choose a restaurant near one of the museums. Mark its location on the street map.

● Locate the Opera Towers Mall on the street map.

Italy

General Information

Web site: http://www.lib.utexas.edu/Libs/PCL/Map_collection/europe/Italy_re186.jpg

- Name three cities you would pass if you traveled east from Milan on a train.
- About how many miles is it from Florence to Rome? What two ways can you travel between the cities?
- Italy is shaped like a boot. Name cities located on the heel and toe of the boot.

Web site: http://www.fromitaly.it/

- Click on the map to visit a **region.** From the regions you can select cities and search out tour and travel information.

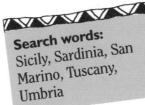

Search words:
Sicily, Sardinia, San Marino, Tuscany, Umbria

Italy

Rome

Web sites: http://www.lonelyplanet.com/dest/eur/graphics/ita1.htm
http://www.lonelyplanet.com/dest/eur/graphics/map-rom.htm

- Enjoy the **Slide Show** of Rome. You may search **Attractions** to discover specifics about these Roman sites. Use the map to locate the landmarks.

Web site: http://www.qni.com/~enj/romekids.htm

- This site provides brief explanations of what children ages ten to seventeen found most interesting about a visit to Rome.
- ✎ Choose one landmark that appeals to you and search for further information on the Internet.

Web site: http://www.cineworld.com/Main/main_screen.html

- Click on **Rome** and view the **walking map** and **sightseeing movie.** Trace a path that takes you to three landmarks.
- Enlarge paintings at Rome's **museums** and locate a **hotel** or **restaurant.**

Italy
Art and Artists
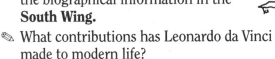

Web site: http://museum.leonardo.net/
- Take a tour of the Leonardo Museum. Enter the **Main Gallery** and choose the area that interests you. Read the biographical information in the **South Wing.**
- ✎ What contributions has Leonardo da Vinci made to modern life?

Web site: http://www.cineworld.com/Main/main_screen.html
- Click on **Florence** and view the **walking map** and **sightseeing movie.** Trace a path that takes you to three landmarks.
- You can enlarge paintings at the **museums** and locate a **hotel** or **restaurant.**

Web site: http://www.michelangelo.com/buonarroti.html
- Read about Michelangelo and click on any of the links to view his artwork.

Italy
Vatican City

Web site: http://www.city.net/vatican_city/
- Enlarge the **Map.** What are the approximate dimensions of St. Peter's Square?
- Click on the **World Fact Book** to determine the size of Vatican City. How is the Vatican different from every other country in the world?
- What is an *enclave?* Do research to find the names of other landmarks in Rome owned by the Vatican.

Web site: http://www.christusrex.org/www1/citta/0-Citta.html
- This site has images of St. Peter's Basilica and the Papal Palace at the Vatican.

Web site: http://www.christusrex.org/www1/sistine/O-Tour.html
- Go to the end of the page and click on **Sistine Chapel** to see a large picture of the interior. You can also see close-ups of the **wall** and **ceiling paintings** and of the **Last Judgement.**
- ✎ What benefits does Italy enjoy because of the location of Vatican City? How does its location inside Rome benefit the Vatican?

Italy
Food

Web sites: http://www.eat.com/places/index.html

http://www.eat.com/pasta-glossary/index.html

● These sites have a clickable **map** with brief information about cities and food of Italy. It provides a good way to compare and contrast local cuisines.

✎ Make a pasta cookbook with pictures and recipes.

Web site: http://www.ghg.net/coyej/history.htm

● Read about the **History of Pizza.** Why is **Pizza Margherita** patriotic?

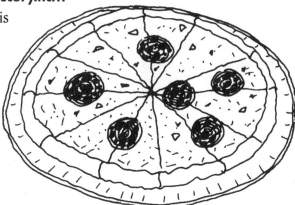

Italy
Archaeology

Web site: http://www.travel.iol.it/tci/english/CAMPANIA/POMPEII.htm

● Locate Pompeii. What major Italian city is nearby? What is Mount Vesuvius? What problem did it cause?

● Describe a typical house in Pompeii.

✎ What have archaeologists learned about early Roman life from their work at Pompeii? What did the people do for work? entertainment?

Web site: http://www.catacombe.roma.it/storia_gb.html

● What are the Catacombs? How did they develop over the years?

● Click on **Map** to locate the Catacombs.

● Click on **Description.** What is a *labyrinth?*

● How were bodies prepared for burial? What was the job of the *fossores?*

✎ Research information about Giovanni Battista de Rossi, the founder of Christian Archaeology.

✎ Search the Internet to find other countries of the world that have catacombs.

Jamaica

General Information

Web site: **http://www.virtualjamaica.com**

● Click on city names for information about specific cities and a **Photo Gallery** for each one. Enlarge the photos to learn about the climate and scenery of Jamaica.

Web site: **http://www.jamaica-irie.com/pictorial/index.html**

● This site has beautiful professional photos of the people, nature, and countryside of Jamaica. Describe the environment.

✎ How is the culture influenced by the beauty of the island?

Web site: **http://www.webcom.com/~travel/jam1.html**

● Use the information to draw a map of Jamaica's terrain.

Web site: **http://www.fantasyisle.com/patois.htm**

● Visit this site to hear a sampling of **Patois,** the language spoken by Jamaicans.

Search words:
reggae, Caribbean, Greater Antilles Islands, ecotourism

Jamaica

Travel and Tourism

Web site: **http://www.fantasyisle.com/map.htm**

● Click on **Kingston,** the capital city, to find attractions to visit.

✎ Choose cities in each area (south, west, north, and east) of the island. Make a chart to show the differences in each area.

✎ Why do most tourists visit Jamaica? Which part of the island would you like to visit? Why?

Web site: **http://www.fantasyisle.com/blus.htm**

● Explain the area around the **Blue Mountains.** What are the peaks? What crop is grown there? Make a diagram of the mountains to show what grows at different levels. Label the cities in the foothills.

Web site: **http://www.info-ascess.com/BluefieldsVillas/map.htm**

● Determine the flying time to Montego Bay, Jamaica, from the city nearest you. Look at a map to determine the route. What cities would you fly over?

✎ Choose five other cities from the list. Trace the path to Jamaica from them.

Japan

General Information ◣◥◣◥◣◥◣◥◣◥◣◥◣◥

Web site: http://lcweb2.loc.gov/frd/cs/jptoc.html

● Read about Japan's **Geographic Regions.** How many islands make up the country? Which island is the largest?

● What factors influence Japan's **Climate?** How does the climate differ in north, central, and southwestern Japan?

● What is the population of Japan? How does it compare to the population of Europe? of the United States?

✎ How does the **Population Density** affect life in Japan?

Web site: http://jw.stanford.edu/KIDS/

● Visit the **Picture Dictionary, Restaurant,** and **School.** Read a Japanese folktale at the **Library.** At these sites you can see Japanese writing and hear the language.

Search words:
Honshu, calligraphy, Hokaido, Okinawa, bonsai

Japan

Fine Arts ◣◥◣◥◣◥◣◥◣◥◣◥◣◥

Web site: http://www.fix.co.jp/kabuki/kabuki.html

● What is unique about **Kabuki** theater? How does it differ from western drama?

● Be sure to visit **Make Up** and the **Online Theater** to get a visual image of Kabuki.

Web site: http://lcweb2.loc.gov/frd/cs/jptoc.html

● What is **Bunraku?** How is it different from Kabuki?

● What **handicrafts** are traditionally Japanese?

Web site: http://www.cjn.or.ip/ukiyo-e/index.html

● Read about the Japanese art form Ukiyo-e (wood block prints) and click on the **Sakai Kokodo Gallery** to view the work. Enlarge the images to see details of nature and Japanese landscapes.

Web sites: http://jw.stanford.edu/KIDS/SCHOOL/ART/kids_arts.html
http://www.supersurf.com/japan/origami.htm

● Practice folding origami in **Arts & Crafts Class.** At these sites you will learn to fold a crane, a *yakko,* or a jumping frog.

Copyright © 1999 Good Year Books

Japan

Holidays and Religion

Web site: http://www.kidlink.org/KIDPROJ/MCC/Japan.html

● Visit the pages of at least five traditional Japanese holidays. How is each one celebrated?

✎ Choose your favorite holiday to picture on a poster.

✎ How are Japanese holidays like or unlike American ones?

Web site: http://www.art.uiuc.edu/tea/main.html

● At this site you can become familiar with the Japanese tea ceremony. Click on **What is the Tea Ceremony?**

✎ What are the four principles of the way of tea? Click on the Japanese characters for authentic photographs. Make a folding book with four pages. Illustrate one principle per page.

Web site: http://www.arts.unimelb.edu.au/fcf/ucr/student/1996/c.parsons/web/shinmore.htm

● Click on **Shinto Terminology** to learn the basic beliefs that dominate Japanese religion. Click on **Shin Shinto** for a photo tour of the Towado Shrine.

✎ What are basic Shinto beliefs? How do these beliefs influence Japanese society?

Japan

Landmarks and Castles

Web site: http://www.magi.com/~ttoyooka/oshiro/

● Click on and enlarge the photos of Japan's many castles. How does Asian construction differ from European? Use the **info page** for locations, details, and additional links for each castle.

✎ Create a map of Japan with the locations marked for each castle.

Web site: http://shrine.cyber.ad.jp/~repka/zvtt.html

● Enjoy a virtual tour of the Tokyo Tower and see interesting aerial views of the city.

Web site: http://www.cs.uidaho.edu/~marc9442/japan.html

● From this site you can see beautiful photos of **Mount Fuji,** Japan's tallest mountain, and the **Peace Parks** at Nagasaki and Hiroshima. Why is each location a significant tourist attraction?

Web site: http://www.mt-fuji.co.jp/index-e.html

● Read **About Mount Fuji** and look at the **Monthly Mt. Fuji** photos. How does the mountain change throughout the year? This site has many clickable photos of Japan's highest peak.

✎ Search the Internet to learn the highest points in five other countries of your choice.

Japan
Tokyo

Web site: http://www.travelchannel.com/spot/japan/top.html
- Here are the **Top Attractions** to see in Tokyo. Choose one to research further.

Web site: http://kiku.stanford.edu/LWT/TOKYO/tokyo_home.html
- Learn about **Tokyo Living.**
- Do you think it would be difficult for an American to adjust to living in the Japanese culture? Explain.

Web site: http://www.tokyodisneyland.co.jp/
- This is the official home page of **Tokyo Disneyland.** What is the price of admission in yen? What refreshments are available? You will find clickable maps at many of the sites.
- How does Tokyo Disneyland compare to an amusement park in the United States?

Web site: http://www.nttls.co.jp/tower/tower.html
- Check this site for a **map** and **realtime photo** of Tokyo. Compare this picture to your city at the same time of day.

Japan
Geography

Web site: http://japan-guide.com/list/e1000.html
- What are Japan's four largest islands? What are the closest neighboring countries?
- What is a **prefecture?** How many prefectures are there in Japan?
- Go to **Earthquakes.** Explain the damage done to Kobe in 1995.
- Make a list of Japan's flora and fauna. Which ones can also be found in the United States?
- Describe a Japanese **raccoon dog.**

Web site: http://www.aist.go.jp/Htmls/Japaninfo/Geography/Geography.html
- At this site you will see graphs and tables comparing the **mountains**, **trenches**, and **rivers** of Japan with those in other countries. You can also find **temperature charts** comparing the range of climate types in cities of the Pacific and the world.
- How would you describe the climate of Tokyo?

Web site: http://www.ceismc.gatech.edu/rasshai/culwww/Flf2.htm
- Click on **Daily Life.** Read the text and questions at the end.
- How would your life be different if you had been born in Japan?

Copyright © 1999 Good Year Books

Kenya

General Information

Web site: http://www.kenyaweb.com/history/history.html
- This site has a very nice pictorial time line of **Kenyan History.** Choose an image and time period that interests you, click on it, and read detailed information.
- ✎ Why is East Africa considered the cradle of humankind?
- ✎ What is the importance of the Mau Mau Rebellion to the Kenyans?

Web site: http://www.bwanazulia.com/kenya/swahili.html
- ✎ Make a Swahili pictionary using the words in this site.

Web site: http://www.odci.gov/cia/publications/nsolo/factbook/ke.htm
- ✎ Make a drawing of the Kenyan flag.
- What countries and bodies of water border Kenya?
- What are Kenya's natural resources?

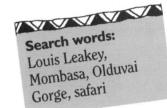

Search words:
Louis Leakey,
Mombasa, Olduvai
Gorge, safari

Web site: http://www.city.net/countries/kenya/nairobi/
- Use this site to determine the **weather** in Nairobi.
- What local craft items are available in Nairobi?

Kenya

Geography

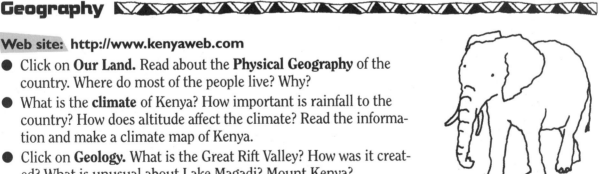

Web site: http://www.kenyaweb.com
- Click on **Our Land.** Read about the **Physical Geography** of the country. Where do most of the people live? Why?
- What is the **climate** of Kenya? How important is rainfall to the country? How does altitude affect the climate? Read the information and make a climate map of Kenya.
- Click on **Geology.** What is the Great Rift Valley? How was it created? What is unusual about Lake Magadi? Mount Kenya?

Web site: http://www.gorp.com/gorp/location/africa/kenya/parkindx.htm
- At this site you can visit some of Kenya's important national parks and wildlife reserves. Some of the best are **Masai Mara, Mount Kenya, The Aberdares,** and **Tsavo.**
- ✎ Make a brief report to the class explaining what a tourist could see and do in a Kenyan wildlife park.

Web site: http://www.bwanazulia.com/kenya/pictures.html
- Enjoy these wonderful **photos** of Kenya. What do they tell you about the climate and terrain of the country?

Korea, South

General Information

Web site: http://falcon.postech.ac.kr/~ipawb/seoul/index_e.html

● Print the eastern and western sections of the map of Seoul. Attach them to make one large map. Where is the Han River?

● How many universities are located in Seoul? Name four cities at the farthest corners (N, S, E, W) of the country.

Web site: http://falcon.postech.ac.kr/~ipawb/index_e.html

● Look at the **Korean Travel Map.** Plan a trip to five cities, beginning and ending at the Seoul airport. Mark the cities on the map. Click on the individual cities for **expressway** maps. Click on **info** to find out what you can see and do in each location.

✎ Write a make-believe travel diary for a five-day stay in Korea.

Web site: http://www.kois.go.kr/overview/overview.html

● At this site you can learn the symbolism of the South Korean flag, see the national flower, and hear the national anthem.

● Who is the current prime minister of South Korea?

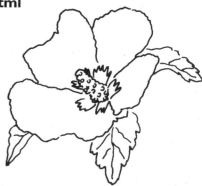

Search words: Cheju Island, North Korea, Pusan, Chong Wa Dae

Korea, South

Seoul

Web site: http://www.metro.seoul.kr/

● Click on **Photo Gallery** to see how Seoul has changed over the years. What is the most obvious difference?

● Click on **Seasonal Customs** to learn about Korean traditions and celebrations.

✎ Make a picture display of the customs observed in the current month. If possible, re-create a Korean tradition in the classroom.

Web site: http://www.city.net/countries/south_korea/seoul/

● Go to **City Guides,** choose **Chung-Gu,** and click on **Famous Sights** and **Cultural Assets.** What do you notice that is unusual or interesting about Korean architecture?

Web site: http://www.chongdong.com

● Visit the Chongdong Theater. Click on **About the Theater,** then **What We Have Performed.** What is important about the Chongdong Theater? What kinds of performances can you see there?

● Look at the subway map. What station is closest to the theater?

Copyright © 1999 Good Year Books

Korea, South
Geography

Web site: http://www.lib.utexas.edu/Libs/PCL/Map_collection/asia.html

- Click on the **Korean Peninsula** map. What bodies of water border North and South Korea? About how many miles is it across the Korean Strait to mainland Japan?
- Locate the line of demarcation between North and South Korea.
- ✎ Research information about life in North Korea. What are the political differences between the two countries?
- Locate Cheju Island. About how many miles is it from the Korean mainland?

Web sites: http://www.kois.go.kr/overview/overview.html
http://korea.emb.washington.dc.us/figures/stat.htm

- What are the seasons in Korea? What are the typical weather conditions of each season?
- What goods are **manufactured** in Korea?

Web site: http://www.kois.go.kr/tourism/

- Click on **Natural Attractions.** Why would a tourist want to visit Korea's beaches, hot springs, and national parks?

Korea, South
Way of Life

Web site: http://www.kois.go.kr/exploring/landplp/thepoeple.html

- What is the ethnic origin of the Korean **people?** Trace their eastward migration on a map.
- Click on **Way of Life.** What is *kimchi?* If you were visiting Korea, would you try it? Explain.
- ✎ Make models or drawings of a traditional Korean house or traditional costumes.
- What are the **major religions** of Korea? Which one has the largest following?
- ✎ Choose one of the religions. Briefly explain its beliefs.
- Explain the levels in the Korean **education** system. How do they differ from schools in the United States?
- Click on **Social Welfare** and read about what the government is doing to solve the housing shortage. Why is there a shortage?
- How has the role of Korean **women** changed in the twentieth century? Look at the chart and read the narrative about employment trends among women. What industry has the most women workers? What industry has the fewest?
- ✎ If you were a Korean woman, what jobs would give you the best opportunity to be successful and earn a living? Explain.

Malaysia

General Information

Web site: **http://www.geocities.com/SiliconValley/Heights/1268/Malaysia.html**

● This site has a basic introduction about Malaysia, its flag, language, and its people.

● What is the *durian?* Draw one.

● What is the significance of the stripes and canton of the flag?

● What are the uses of the *bunga raya?*

Web site: **http://asiatravel.com/malinfo.html**

● What is the population and capital city of Malaysia?

● Make a calendar showing the national holidays and festivals of Malaysia. Do research to find the dates of "movable feasts."

● What is the general climate in Malaysia?

Web site: **http://sunsite.nus.sg/SEAlinks/maps/malaysia.gif**

● What countries border Malaysia? Explain the location of Brunei.

● About how many miles is Malaysia from Miri and Bintula?

Search words:
Malay (language),
Kuala Lumpur,
Brunei, Borneo,
Penang Island

Malaysia

States

Web site: **http://arkib.gov.my/**

● Click on **Photographs** and view twelve exhibits of Malaysian history.

✎ Print several files and cut apart the pictures to make a collage. Include a map and flag in the center of your project.

Web site: **http://www.jaring.my/stb/**

● Where is **Sarawak** located? How many **Ethnic Groups** are living there? Read the information and trace the immigration patterns of the Iban, Chinese, Melanau, and Bidayuh people.

✎ What differences do you notice in the traditional clothing of each group? Make labeled drawings of the head coverings of each group.

Web site: **http://www.jaring.my/sabah/**

● Click on **Nature and Wildlife** and then **Sandakan** to read about the diverse wildlife present in the rain forests of Sabah. How is the government protecting the **Oran Utan?**

● What is the **Rafflesia?** How is it reproduced?

● What would you learn from a **longhouse** visit?

✎ Make drawings to show your adventure.

Malaysia
Travel and Tourism

Web site: http://asiatravel.com/malinfo.html

● How do people travel within the country? Considering the economy and climate, what method of travel is best for a tourist? a citizen?

Web site: http://www.lonelyplanet.com/dest/sea/graphics/map-emal.htm

● Use the interactive maps of **Peninsular Malaysia** and **Eastern Malaysia** to create your own map showing the main tourist attraction in each area.

● Look at the **Slide Show.** What do you see that lets you know Malaysia is a Muslim country?

Web sites: http://asiatravel.com/kuainfo.html
http://www.regit.com/malaysia/intplace/kl/kl.htm

● Read the information and then write a paragraph about shopping in Kuala Lumpur. Where are the shopping districts? What is available? How can you be sure of getting a bargain?

● Click on **Spectacular Sights** and make a list of five places that interest you. Search the Internet for additional information about those places.

✎ Make a travel poster advertising points of interest in Kuala Lumpur.

Malaysia
Geography

Web site: http://www.odci.gov/cia/publications/nsolo/factbook/my.htm

● What are the geographic coordinates of Malaysia?
● To what U.S. state is it similar in size?
● What are Malaysia's natural resources?

✎ Deforestation is an environmental concern in Malaysia. Read the information in **Economy** to find out what industries threaten Malaysia's forests. Considering the future, how might deforestation impact the tourist business?

Web site: http://www.interknowledge.com/malaysia/

● At this site you can see photos of the country. Click on **Islands and Beaches.** What general statements can you make about the climate, flora and fauna, and terrain of these islands?

✎ Do you think it is in Malaysia's best interest to keep areas like these undeveloped? Explain.

● Click on **Culture and People.** Explain the Malay wedding ceremony.

● Go to **Games and Pastimes.** How do the Malay people spend their leisure time? How are these activities similar to ones enjoyed in the United States?

Mexico

General Information

Web sites: http://www.wtgonline.com/info.html
http://www.lonelyplanet.com.au/dest/cam/graphics/map-mex.htm

- Choose **Mexico** and read the geography section.
- Locate Mexico on a map of the world and label the bordering countries and bodies of water. Label the main agricultural region of the country and the Sierra Madre Occidental Mountain Range.
- Click on **climate.** Read the information and design symbols for a climate map of Mexico. What months make up the dry and wet seasons?

Web site: http://mexico.udg.mx/Ingles/Historia/datos.html

- Use the time line of Mexican history to answer these questions:
  When did the Spanish arrive in Tenochtitlán?
  When was the War for Independence?
  What did General Porfirio Diaz do to and for the country?
  What is the importance of the GATT Treaty to Mexico?

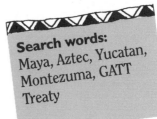

Search words:
Maya, Aztec, Yucatan, Montezuma, GATT Treaty

Mexico

Archaeological Sites

Web site: http://www.sci.mus.mn.us/sln/ma/sites.html

- Explore **Chichén Itzá,** the **Great City,** and the **Cenotes.** Look at the stonework in the architecture.
- What does the stonework tell you about the craftsmen of Chichén Itzá?

Web sites: http://www.iminet.com/mexico/zchiruin.html
http://www.hotwired.com/rough/mexico/southern.states/chiapas/

- Search the Mayan ruins in Chiapas. Read the general information, and locate Palenque on a map of Mexico.
- Do further reseach on the Mayan people. Make a map showing the areas where they lived. What kinds of homes did they build?

Web site: http://pharos.bu.edu/Egypt/Wonders/Natural/paricutin.html

- Look at photos of the volcano. Click on related sites and learn what makes this volcano unique.
- Click on **Images of Volcanoes** to see other volcanoes in South America.

Mexico

Travel and Tourism

Web site: http://www.mextnet.com/index.htm
- Click on **Destinations.** What can a tourist expect to see and do at a Mexican hotel?
- Click on **Travel Tips.** What can you do to assure a safe and healthful trip?

Web site: http://www.hotwired.com/rough/mexico/mexico.and.around/
- Read about the basics of where to eat and sleep while in Mexico City. What can you expect to pay for one night in an average hotel?
- When should you eat your main meal of the day?

Web site: http://www.iminet.com/mexico/ecolun.html
- Read about **Ecotourism** in Mexico at several locations. Choose one destination to search fully. What would you learn from a trip like this? How does ecotourism benefit Mexico?
- ✎ How would you interest someone in taking an ecotourism vacation instead of a beach holiday? What are the benefits of each?

Mexico

Travel and Tourism

Web site: http://www.wotw.com/mexico/
- Print a **map** of **Mexico's major cities.** Choose five cities to visit on a two-week virtual vacation. Select a hotel in each city from the main menu.
- What craft items could you expect to find in each location?

Web site: http://www.go2mexico.com/
- Search this clickable map of Mexico's best tourist attractions.
- Go to **Copper Canyon.** How do visitors see the canyons? What Indians live there?

Web site: http://www.mexonline.com/
- What entry requirements must you meet before crossing the border into Mexico? What personal items should you take along to ensure a pleasant visit?

Web site: http://www.go2mexico.com/
- Go to **Spanish Helper.**
- ✎ Practice common phrases in Spanish. Try asking and answering several questions with a partner.

Mexico

Culture and Cuisine

Web site: http://www.diegorivera.com/

● Visit the **Gallery** of one of Mexico's most famous painters. What is his style of painting? What are his most common subjects?

● Click on **Biography** for a time line of the artist's life. Where have his works been exhibited outside of Mexico?

Web site: http://www.mexonline.com/mexfood.htm

● This site has a extensive glossary of Mexican foods.

✎ Use the information to develop a simple menu in Spanish. Learn to say the Spanish words for your favorite foods.

Mexico

Aztecs and Mayas

Web site: http://www.indians.org/welker/mexman01.htm

● This site has information about the **Indigenous Nations of Mexico.** What is the origin of the name *Mexico?*

● Read about the **Aztecs** who lived in the Valley of Mexico around the fourteenth century.

✎ Research information and write a report about the Aztec city of Tenochtitlán. What stands on its location today?

Web site: http://www.mecc.com/maya97/maya/maya.html

● Read information about the **Ancient** and **Modern Empires.** What regions of Mexico have been home to the old and new Maya?

● In what years did the Maya flourish?

● Where do the Maya live today?

● Read additional information about **Mayan Archaeology.**

● What do archaeologists believe was the reason for the collapse of Mayan civilization?

● Click on **Images** for a quick slide show from MayaQuest.

Monaco

General Information

Web site: http://www.monaco.mc/monaco/guide_en.html

- Click on **General Information** and learn the distances between Monaco and several important European cities. Mark the routes on a map.
- Click on **History.** When did Prince Ranier III ascend the throne? In what year was he married? Whom did he marry? In what years were their three children born?
- ✎ How did Princess Grace die?

Web site: http://www.odci.gov/cia/publications/nsolo/factbook/mn.htm

- Monaco's **economy** is very successful. What is the main source of income? What is the average per capita income?
- What products are manufactured in Monaco?
- In case of attack, what country will defend Monaco?
- ✎ If you were interested in moving to Monaco, what would be a good business to establish? Why?

Search words:
Grimaldi, Fontvieille,
French Riviera,
Monegasque

Monaco

Geography

Web site: http://www.lib.utexas.edu/Libs/PCL/Map_collection/europe/Monaco.jpg

- This map is drawn to scale in feet and meters because Monaco is very small. About how far is it from one end of the principality to the other? How long would it take you to walk that distance?
- What European countries border Monaco?

Web sites: http://www.odci.gov/cia/publications/nsolo/factbook/mn.htm
http://www.wtgonline.com/country/mc/gen.html

- What are the geographic coordinates of Monaco?
- What two countries have flags similar to that of Monaco?
- What is the total land area of Monaco?
- How many people live in Monaco?
- What natural resources does Monaco have?
- What is the official language?
- How would you describe the climate?

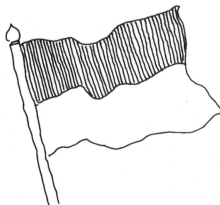

Monaco

Travel and Tourism

Web site: http://www.monaco.mc/monaco/click/click.html
- Use the **clickable map** to view the natural beauty of Monaco. Enlarge the photos to full screen. How would you describe the terrain and climate of Monaco?

Web site: http://www.monaco.mc/monaco/gprix
- The **Monaco Grand Prix** draws many visitors each year. Click on the image map to see photos taken along the track of the April 1997 race.
- ✎ Research the kinds of cars that race in the Grand Prix.

Web site: http://www.visiteurope.com/
- Click on Monaco.
- Read about things to do and see in Monaco. About how large is the principality?
- Click on **Activities** to read about entertainment, cuisine, and shopping in Monaco.
- ✎ Click on **Practical Information** and send for a free booklet about travel in Monaco.

Monaco

History, Government, and Culture

Web site: http://www.monaco.mc/ind_toc.html
- Make a list of museums in Monaco. Indicate what is exhibited at each one.
- ✎ Read the information in **700 years of the Grimaldi's** in Web site and create a time line showing the important events in Monaco's history.
- Explain the symbolism of the official logo.

Web site: http://www.monaco.mc/monaco/info/acult.html
- Read about the **Great Cultural Institutions** of Monaco. What general statement might describe them all? Is the emphasis on art or music? How does this cultural atmosphere influence life in the principality?

Morocco

General Information

Web site: http://www.odci.gov/cia/publications/nsolo/factbook/mo.htm

- What is the significance of the star on the Moroccan flag?
- What is Morocco's capital city?
- Who is the current chief of state?

Web site: http://www.wtgonline.com/country/ma/cc.html

- Study the **climate chart.** Write three general statements about the temperature, rainfall, and humidity in Rabat, Morocco.

Web site: http://www.wtgonline.com/country/ma/gen.html

- Read the **history** of Morocco. Answer these questions:
  What countries first colonized the area?
  When did it become independent?
  Who was the first head of state?

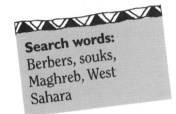

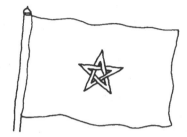

Search words:
Berbers, souks, Maghreb, West Sahara

Morocco

Cities

Web site: http://www.maghreb.net/countries/morocco/cities.html

- Click on **Marrakech** to read about the crafts that are sold at public markets. Choose **Jemaa el Fna Square** and make a list of people who sell their services (rather than goods).
- Make a sketch map of the market at Jemaa el Fna Square.
- Read about the importance of **Casablanca,** Morocco's largest city. What goods are manufactured in the factories of Casablanca? How will the city change in the twenty-first century?
- How does **Tangier** differ from Casablanca or Marrakech?
- Read about two other Moroccan cities. Of the five cities you have studied, which would you most like to visit? Explain.

Morocco

People

Web site: http://www.arab.net/morocco/culture/mo_people.html
- Read about the Arab-Berber people, the major ethnic group in Morocco. How long have the Berbers lived in North Africa? What is their primary occupation?
- What languages are spoken in Morocco?

Web site: http://www.maghreb.net/countries/morocco/culture.html
- Click on **Handicrafts.** How has technology affected the craft business?
- What is a *souk?* What handicrafts are available?

Web site: http://www.odci.gov/cia/publications/nsolo/factbook/mo.htm
- What is the life expectancy of Moroccan men? women?
- What is the birthrate?
- What is Morocco's main religion?

Morocco

Geography

Web site: http://www.sas.upenn.edu/African_Studies/CIA_Maps/Morocco_19858.gif
- About how far is it from Tangier to the coast of Spain? How would you get there?
- About how many miles would you travel along the coast between Casablanca and Tangier?
- What are the geographic coordinates of Marrakech?

Web site: http://www.odci.gov/cia/publications/nsolo/factbook/mo.htm
- On what continent is Morocco? What countries and bodies of water mark its boundaries?
- What is the relationship between West Sahara and Morocco?
- Where is the Strait of Gibraltar?

Web site: http://www.arab.net/morocco/morocco_contents.html
- Morocco has an **agricultural economy.** What are its chief crops and livestock?
- What products does Morocco **export** and **import?**

Netherlands

General Information

Web site: http://www.lib.utexas.edu/Libs/PCL/Map_collection/europe/
Netherlands.jpg

● What is the capital city of the Netherlands?
● What countries border the Netherlands? Where is the North Sea?
✎ Make a map that shows five major cities and the inland waterways.

Web site: http://www.proqc.com/~jeroen/main.html

● Create a time line of Netherlands history. Include information about
trading companies, the French Revolution, and the world wars.
● Click on **Facts** and read about the land and resources of the country.
What is a *polder?* How much of the country lies below sea level?
How have the people managed to avoid regular flooding?

Search words:
Netherlands Antilles,
Aruba, Holland,
Zeeland, Flevoland,
The Hague

Web sites: http://www.nbt.nl/trad-kinderdijk.html
http://www.nbt.nl/trad-millmus.html
http://www.regionlink.com/north-holland/tourist/english/emolens.htm

● View some windmill photos. Read about the windmill museums.
✎ Make a diagram to illustrate how the Dutch reclaim their land from the sea.

Netherlands

Amsterdam

Web site: http://www.cineworld.com

● Select **Amsterdam** and then go to **Sightseeing Movie** and **Panoramas** for images of the canals and
the homes built along them.
● What characteristics make Dutch architecture unique?

Web site: http://www.city.net/countries/netherlands/amsterdam/

● What will the weather be in Amsterdam this week?

Web sites: http://www.channels.nl/amsterdam/annefran.html
http://www.annefrank.com/

● These sites offer in-depth information about Anne Frank. The
house where she hid is in Amsterdam. What family members
were with her? What was her ultimate fate?
✎ Read a portion of Anne Frank's diary. How do you think you
would have reacted to a similar circumstance?

Netherlands

Artists and Museums

Web sites: http://www.cineworld.com/
http://www.gallery-guide/gg/museum/vangogh/index.htm
http://www.rembrandthuis.nl/

● Select **Amsterdam** and then go to **Museums.** From this site you will be able to click on and enlarge several works of Van Gogh and Rembrandt at museums dedicated to their artwork.

✎ Compare and contrast the works of these two famous Dutch artists in a Venn diagram.

Web site: http://http://museon.museon.nl/contents.html

● Take this guided tour through the permanent exhibition at the science museum at The Hague.

Web site: http://amsterdam.park.org:8888/Netherlands/pavilions/food_and_markets/
cheese/museum.html

● At this site you will read about three cheese museums. What artifacts are on display?

✎ Locate a recipe for a cheese snack that you can prepare at home and share with the class.

Netherlands

Culture and Tradition

Web site: http://www.regionlink.com/north-holland/tourist/english/eprovnh.htm

● Read the information to find out what products make Noord-Holland famous.

● Click on **Flowers.** What flowers are grown in the region?

✎ Research how each of the Dutch flowers is grown in the United States.

● Click on **Recreation on the Water.** What water sports are common?

Web site: http://www.nbt.nl/cast-muiderslot.html

● Read about the **Muiderslot** and **Loevenstein Castles.** Locate them on a map of the Netherlands.

Web site: http://www.nbt.nl/trad-index.html

● Why did Dutch farmers begin wearing **wooden shoes?**

● Describe the regional costumes of the Netherlands. When do the people wear this style of **traditional dress?**

Web site: http://amsterdam.park.org:8888/Netherlands/pavilions/food_and_markets/

● Click on **Cheese** and read information about the making of Edam, Leyden, and Gouda. Locate the cities where they are made on a map of the Netherlands.

New Zealand

General Information

Web site: http://city.net/countries/new_zealand/maps/

- Enlarge and print the maps. Locate the main cities of New Zealand.
- Describe in your own words information about the geographic makeup of New Zealand, its discovery, and the native people.

Web site: http://www.nz.com/NZ/Geography/

- Click on **volcanoes in New Zealand.** Use the clickable map to get specific information about different locations. The home page explains how volcanoes are formed.

Web site: http://www.nz.com/NZ/Culture/

- Select the **New Zealand-English Dictionary** and learn several variations on English words and phrases that New Zealanders use.
- ✎ Write a short story substituting New Zealand's English whenever possible. Read your story to the class.
- Listen to the **National Anthem.**

Search words:
Cook Islands, Tokelau, Niue, Aotearoa, Stewart Islands

New Zealand

Travel and Tourism

Web site: http://www.akiko.lm.com/tour/

- Select a virtual **tour** of Auckland or of the North or South Islands. In addition, view the **Slide Shows** at this site. What do these slides tell you about the terrain and climate of New Zealand?

Web site: http://www.nz.com/tour/Auckland/

- Select **Sights** and read about what a tourist can see and do in Auckland.

Web site: http://www.nz.com/tour/Wellington/

- Click on **Sights** and compare the attractions with those in Auckland.

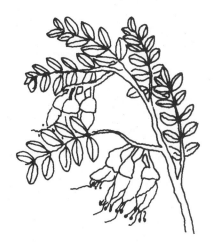

New Zealand

North Island

Web site: http://www.akiko.lm.com/tour/NorthIsland.html

- At this site you will learn about many cities on the **North Island.**
- Select **Auckland.** Why is it called the **City of Sails?**
- Select **Rotorua.** The geothermal areas are among the finest in the world. This city also is the center of **Maori Culture.**
- Do research to understand what causes the geysers, fumaroles, and hot pools in this region.
- Select **Wellington,** then **History.** When and why was it chosen as New Zealand's capital city?

Web sites: http://www.maori.org.nz/

http://www.lonelyplanet.com.au/dest/aust/maori.html

- Who are the Maori people? At these sites you can read their history, learn about their customs, view their crafts, and hear their music.

New Zealand

South Island

Web site: http://www.akiko.lm.com/tour/SouthIsland.html

- At this site you will learn about many cities on the **South Island.**
- Read the information about **Dunedin.** Who founded the city? What makes the city unique?
- Click on the **Otago Peninsula Slide Show.** Locate the peninsula on a map of New Zealand. What wildlife makes its home there?
- Search the Internet for a picture of an albatross. What is its natural habitat?
- What would you see on a visit to **glacier** country? Name the two principle glaciers in South Westland.
- Where is **Queenstown** located? What features make it the most popular tourist destination in New Zealand?
- What is **Fiordland?**
- Describe the environment on **Stewart Island.**

Nigeria
General Information

Web site: http://www.city.net/countries/nigeria/maps/
- What is the geographic location of Abuja, Nigeria's capital?
- In what region of the African continent is Nigeria located?
- What countries border Nigeria?
- Name three cities on the Niger River.

Web sites: http://www.city.net/countries/nigeria/
http://www.wtgonline.com/country/ng/gen.html
- What **disease** poses a major health risk in Nigeria?
- Is Nigeria a popular tourist destination? Explain.
- What is the **official language** of Nigeria?
- What **clothing** is appropriate for the south of Nigeria during the rainy season? the north during December and January?

Web site: http://edcen.ehhs.cmich.edu/wcp/page10.html
- Listen to recordings of the **Hausa** language.

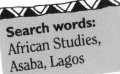

Search words:
African Studies,
Asaba, Lagos

Nigeria
Environment

Web site: http://www.irn.org/irn/nigeria/ekuri.html
- What is the purpose of the Ekuri Initiative? What has the community done to help save the forests?

Web site: http://www.wtgonline.cpm/country/ng/gen.html
- Click on **Climate.** Explain how the climate varies among areas. Which region is most likely to experience a drought?
- Select **Climate Charts**. Which of the three cities has the lowest rainfall amounts and highest temperatures?
- ✎ How would the growing season be influenced by this concentrated rainfall?

Web sites: http://www.shellnigeria.com/video/photo.html
http://europe.shellnigeria.com/video/ClipC.html
- Look at photos of the Community, Environment, and Shell Facilities in Nigeria.
- Click on **About Shell in Nigeria**. Read about the impact of oil drilling on the people and the environment.
- ✎ What are the pros and cons of oil exploration in countries like Nigeria? What could be done to lessen the negative impact? Who should be responsible?

Norway

General Information

Web site: **http://www.odci.gov/cia/publications/nsolo/factbook/no.html**
- What is the total area of Norway? What countries does it border? Describe the **terrain.**
- What are Norway's **natural resources?**
- What is the main **religion** of Norwegians?
- Who is the **U.S. ambassador** to Norway? What is his or her address?

Web site: **http://www.lonelyplanet.com.au/dest/eur/nor.htm**
- Click on **Slide Show** to see typical village homes of Norway.

Web site: **http://www.troll.no/trolls.html**
- Click on **Th. Kittelsen** (the artist's name) for an in-depth look at real Norwegian trolls. Choose one of the trolls and describe its appearance in detail.

Web site: **http://www.uit.no/planetarium**
- Take a virtual tour of the **Northern Lights Planetarium.** What causes the aurora borealis?

> **Search words:**
> Scandinavia, Vikings, Oslo, trolls

Norway

Travel and Tourism

Web site: **http://www.intercom.no/travel/map/**
- Use this clickable **map** to visit **Fjord Norway.** What is a *fjord?* Look at the photos. What would draw a tourist to this area?

Web site: **http://home.sol.no/~mariushe/nor/climb_ guide_norway.hmtl**
- Tourists enjoy hiking, skiing, climbing, and cycling in these mountains. Name three climbing areas.
- Describe the climate in the mountains.
- ✎ Make a list of equipment you would need to take the outdoor vacation of your choice.
- ✎ Search the Internet to learn more about Sognefjord.

Web site: **http://www.monet.no/hr/us/**
- Click on **Journey** and enjoy the world's most beautiful cruise. From the picture page, click on the **land of contrasts.** Read the information and explain in your own words what is old and new about Norway.
- ✎ If you were visiting Norway, would you prefer to take a cruise or climb a mountain? Explain your choice.

Norway
Vikings

Web site: http://www.pastforward.co.uk/vikings/

● Visit the Borg Viking Museum in Norway. Click on **Wealth of Finds** and **Reconstructions from Viking Times.**

✎ Make a drawing of the chieftain's kitchen and banquet hall.

✎ What is *Lofotr?*

✎ Search the Internet for names and pictures of other Viking ships.

Web site: http://www.netgravity.com/employees/jk/pix/norway/index/html

● Learn more about the Vikings at the **Bygdoy Museums** in Oslo.

● Explain how the *Oseberg* ship was found. What was found on that ship?

✎ Use what you've learned to make a drawing of a ship labeled with technical terms.

Norway
Environment

Web site: http://www.rri.org/envatlas/europe/norway/no-index.html

● Read the **background information** on the environment. What are the **Special Areas of Concern?**

● Click on **International Cooperation** and explain how factors outside Norway's borders threaten its environment.

✎ With what countries does Norway have treaties for common cleanup of oil spills or radioactive waste?

Web site: http://www.grida.no/soeno95/

● Click on **Urban Environmental Quality.** What is the most important source of air and noise pollution in Norway? What time of the year is pollution the worst? Explain.

● Click on **Cultural and Natural Landscapes.** How are humans altering the natural landscape of Norway? What effect will this have on the country in general?

● How do Norwegians plan to reduce **Waste** in their country?

✎ What kinds of waste occur? What are the negative effects? How are Norway's problems with waste similar to those in the United States?

Panama

General Information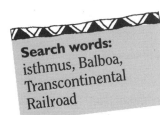

Web site: http://holly.colostate.edu/~panama/panama.html

- Click on links for information about the **history** of Panama. How was the isthmus of Panama probably formed? What artifacts have been found from early civilizations?
- How did the California gold rush change Panama?

Web site: http://www.odci.gov/cia/publications/nsolo/factbook/pm.htm

- Draw the flag of Panama.
- What are Panama's chief agricultural and industrial products?
- What is the population of Panama? How is the population divided, by age? by gender?

Web site: http://holly.colostate.edu/~panama/section6.html

- Read about the **Culture of Panama.** What is a *mola?* Describe the Panamanian women's national dress. What dishes would you order at a Panamanian restaurant?

Search words:
isthmus, Balboa, Transcontinental Railroad

Panama

Geography

Web site: http://www.odci.gov/cia/publications/nsolo/factbook/pm.htm

- Why is the geographic location of Panama significant to the United States? How does its location affect the economy of the country? What percentage of the labor force works in service industries?

Web site: http://holly.colostate.edu/~panama/section7.html

- Read the background of the Panama Canal and details about its construction. Why was the canal important as a trade route?
- In what direction would you travel from your home to Panama? What transportation would you use? What major cities would you pass through or fly over?

Web site: http://holly.colostate.edu/~panama/section5.html

- Take a look at the **interior** of Panama. How is life different on the Azuero Peninsula? What agricultural products are grown? What is significant about the city of Contadora?
- Locate five interior cities on a map of Panama.

Philippines
General Information

Web site: http://www.wtgonline.com/country/ph/gen.html

- What is the capital city of the Philippines? What is the population?
- How many islands and islets make up the Philippines? Name the two largest islands.
- What is the most important religion?
- Read the **History** section. What groups of people were the earliest inhabitants? Who claimed the islands for Spain? Who was Ferdinand Marcos?

Web site: http://www.jake.com/DIVE/locker.html

- Enjoy **Diving in the Philippines.** What makes the Philippines a diver's paradise?
- Use the clickable **Dive Map** for specific sites and resorts.
- View the images in the **Photo Gallery.**
- ✎ Choose a location to search in depth, or make a pictionary of sea life native to the Philippines.

Search words:
Filipino, Pangasinan, archipelago

Philippines
Geography

Web site: http://www.wtgonline.com/country/ph/gen.html

- Click and print the **Map Page.** Label the seven central islands.
- Click on **Climate.** What clothing is appropriate year-round?
- ✎ What is a *typhoon?* What parts of the world experience typhoons?

Web site: http://www.sino.net/asean/philippn.html

- Explain in your own words the **terrain** of the Philippines.
- ✎ How are islands created from extinct volcanoes?

Web site: http://www.geo.mtu.edu/~mtdolan/pinatubo/volcano/pinatubo.volcano

- Enlarge a series of photos of the volcano (Mount Pinatubo). Is Mount Pinatubo an active volcano at present?

Poland

General Information

Web site: http://www.lib.utexas.edu/Libs/PCL/Map_collection/europe/Poland.jpg

● What is the approximate distance between Warsaw, Poland, and Prague, Czech Republic?
● What body of water must you cross to travel from Gdansk, Poland, to Denmark or Sweden?

Web sites: http://werple.mira.net.au/~margaret/poland.htm
http://www.lonelyplanet.com.au/dest/eur/pol.htm

● These are the best places to see the **Sights of Poland**.
● Describe the terrain and climate of Poland by making two maps.

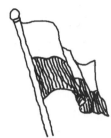

Web site: http://www.travel.com.pl/stuff/info.html

● What products does Poland **export** and **import?**
● What percentage of the **labor force** works in agriculture? industry?
● Read the **culture** section. How have religion and Communism influenced Polish art?
✎ Make a list of characteristic Polish foods that you have eaten.

Search words:
Polska, Silesia, Lech Walesa, Baltic Sea, Communism, Socialism

Poland

Castles and Cities

Web site: http://www.explore-poland.pl/guide/index.html

● From this site you can visit many of Poland's **cities and towns**.
✎ Choose ten cities and make a chart to show their major attractions.

Web sites: http://hum.amu.edu.pl/~gmazurek/zpd/zpden.htm
http://www.poland.net/castles/

● This site presents information about castle history as well as summaries and links to photos. Many of the castles house museums and have extensive gardens.
✎ Locate ten castles on a map of Poland.

Web site: http://citynet4.excite.com/countries/poland/krakow/

● Click on the **city guide,** then **Tourism** for a tour of Cracow. (Krakow) Click on **one day in Cracow** to see and read about highlights of the city.

Web site: http://citynet4.excite.com/countries/poland/warsaw/

● Click on **Warsaw weather**. What is the five-day forecast? What kind of clothing should you take to visit this time of year?

Poland

Famous People

Web site: http://werple.mira.net.au/~margaret/chopin.htm

- How does Frédéric Chopin use references to Poland in his piano music? Click on a link to hear a mazurka or polonaise.
- Research additional information about the life and piano music of this great composer.

Web site: http://www-groups.dcs.st-and.ac.uk/history/Mathematicians/Copernicus.html

- Use any of the links for biographical information about **Nicolaus Copernicus.** Locate his birthplace on a map of Poland. What was his education? What careers did he follow?
- Make a drawing of Copernicus's sun-centered solar system.

Web site: http://www.nobel.se/laureates/peace-1983-1-bio.html

- Read the biography of **Lech Walesa.** How did he lead the Polish workers? What award did he win in 1983? When did he serve as president of Poland?
- Search the Internet to find the name of Poland's current leader.

Poland

Environment

Web site: http://hum.amu.edu.pl/~zbzw/ph/pnp/pnp.htm

- What is the main task of the **National Parks?** Use the clickable map to locate them.
- Make a chart that indicates the parks' flora and fauna.

Web site: http://ciesin.ci.uw.edu.pl/poland/environmentintro.html

- What forms of pollution threaten the Polish environment?
- What can people do to improve and protect their environment?

Web site: http://www.lonelyplanet.com.au/dest/eur/pol.htm

- Click on **environment.** How much of the country is covered by forests?

Web sites: http://www.cs.put.poznan.pl/holidays/tatry/
http://www.infocom.net/~romanm/tatry.html

- Locate the Carpathian Mountain Range on a map of Europe. Where are the Tatra Mountains?
- Which section of the Tatras is most popular with tourists?
- Draw a map that shows the Tatra Mountains and the two countries in which they are located.

Russian Federation

General Information

Web site: http://www.wtgonline.com/country/ru/gen.html

● What is the population of the Russian Federation?

● Read the historical information. Who were the first immigrants? Who was the first tsar? Who was the first Bolshevik leader?

● Click on **Climate.** Use the information to design climate maps for summer and winter.

Web site: http://mars.uthscsa.edu/Russia/200.html

● What does Russia **export? import?**

● What countries are Russia's trade **partners?**

✎ How would the Russian economy improve with increased trade?

Web site: http://www.b-info.com/places/Bulgaria/cyr/

● Read information about the development of the Cyrillic alphabet used in the Russian language. Why would it be difficult to learn to read and write this language?

Search words:
Karl Marx, Anastasia, Siberia, Boris Yeltsin, Mikhail Gorbachev, Bolshevik, Crimea

АБВГДЄЖZ РСТ& ЮА

Russian Federation

Geography

Web site: http://mars.uthscsa.edu/Russia/200.html

● What is the **total land area** of Russia? How much larger is Russia than the United States?

✎ Make a topographical map showing the Ural Mountains, the Siberian tundra, and the steppes in the south. Indicate the line between European and Asian Russia. Label the border countries.

Web site:
http://www.lib.utexas.edu/Libs/PCL/Map_collection/commonwealth/Russian_Env96.jpg

● Use this map to identify **environmental problem areas** of Russia.

✎ List Russia's environmental concerns. What areas have been dump sites for radioactive waste? Where are degraded forests?

✎ What part of the country is relatively clear of pollution? Why is this?

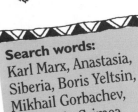

Web site: http://www.abisnet.com/buryatia4.htm

● This site has information about Lake Baikal, the world's deepest freshwater lake. Go to **Background** and then **Baikal Facts** to read statistics of the lake. Locate Lake Baikal on a map.

✎ How was the lake formed? Why is it said that Baikal has "living water"? How does Baikal compare in size to the Great Lakes of the United States?

Russian Federation

Cities

Web site: http://redsun.cs.msu.su/

- Click on the **Moscow Guide.** Select **Overview** to learn the location and climate of the Russian capital.
- How many **people** live in greater Moscow?
- What is their major **religion?**
- View the clickable images from the Moscow and St. Petersburg **Photo Gallery**.

Web site: http://www.lonelyplanet.com/dest/eur/mos.htm

- Use the interactive **map** of Moscow to locate attractions and plan a walking tour. Read the information about **Attractions** and describe to a travel partner what you will see in Moscow.

Web sites: http://www.lonelyplanet.com/dest/eur/stp.htm
http://www.friends-partners.org/partners/asebrant/life/1996/sept-spb.html

- What is unique about the planning and construction of St. Petersburg? What ruler designed the city? What river divides the city into sections?
- Look at the **Slide Show.** Describe the architecture of Russian churches.

Russian Federation

Past, Present, and Future

Web site: http://www.times.st-pete.fl.us/Treasures/TC.2.3.html

- This site provides a **time line** covering four centuries of the Romanov dynasty. Click on **1900s** and read about Nicholas II, the last emperor of Russia. What events led to his abdication? What was his fate?
- Take the **Museum Tour** to experience the art and artifacts of Russia. Choose an item of clothing or armor to describe in detail.

Web site: http://www.friends-partners.org/partners/asebrant/life/ml.html

- This site will give you a good idea of daily life in Moscow. Read the stories this family has recorded since 1995.
- How is Russian life most different from life in the United States? What would you enjoy about living in Russia? What do you believe is most difficult for the citizens of Russia?

Web site: http://www.f8.com/FP/Russia/Wschdir.html

- Read **messages to the world** about the future from twelve Russian schoolchildren. What are their hopes for the future?
- If you would like to ask a question or make a comment, you can send e-mail by clicking **Mailbox.**

Russian Federation
Landmarks

Web site: http://www.midwinter.com/~koreth/russia/kremlin/
- At this site you can see clickable photos of the Kremlin. Go to the **List of Places** and see points of interest around Moscow and St. Petersburg.

Web site: http://www.interknowledge.com/russia
- Select **Moscow** and then the **Kremlin** for a detailed description of its buildings and grounds.
- ✎ Compare the Kremlin and the Tower of London on a Venn diagram.
- What historic events took place on **Red Square?** What is GUM? How is Lenin's body displayed?
- Click on **St. Petersburg** and then the **Hermitage,** one of Russia's finest museums. What does the museum hold? How does it compare to the Louvre in Paris, France?
- What **Historical Sites** can be seen in St. Petersburg? What is the story of the Bronze Horseman?

Russian Federation
Fine Arts

Web site: http://www.webwin.com/tourism/sydney/attracts/power/faberge/exhibition.html
- At this site read information and click on links to see three Fabergé eggs. For whom were the eggs made? What precious metals and jewels were used?
- ✎ Search for additional information and images of Fabergé creations on the Internet.

Web site: http://www.odyssey.net/subscribers/scior/pit.html
- At this site you can hear excerpts from the music of Peter Ilich Tchaikovsky, Russia's most famous composer of classical music. Click on **Biographical Info** and use the time line to write a brief biography about his life.

Web site: http://www.nobunaga.demon.co.uk/htm/ruscomp.htm
- ✎ Research information about other famous Russian composers: Alexander Borodin, Nikolai Rimsky-Korsakov, Sergei Prokofiev, and Modest Mussorgsky. Read the links. List one composition written by each man.

Saudi Arabia

General Information

Web site: http://ale.physics.sunysb.edu/~rreese/Saudi/saudi1.html
- This site has a fine set of photos introducing the Saudi people and their homeland. How would you describe the style of architecture? dress?

Web site: http://www.saudi.net/mainpage.html
- Click on **Profile** and read information about Saudi history, religion, government, and economy.
- Read the **History** of the kingdom. Who were the early inhabitants of the Arabian Peninsula? How did these people contribute to the Greek and Roman civilizations?
- How was the lifestyle of early Arabs influenced by life in the desert?

Web site: http://www.saudi.net/multimedia/multimedia.html
- View a large set of photos on every phase of Saudi life. Click on the photos to enlarge.
- Print a set of photos that represent the historical, leisure-time, religious, and business interests of the kingdom.

Web site: http://www.arab.net/saudi
- Click on **Business** and then **Economy.** What exports dominate the Saudi economy?

Search words:
desalination plant, Bedouin, Makkah, Persian Gulf

Saudi Arabia

Geography

Web site: http://www.arab.net/saudi
- Click on **Map.** What is different about the map of Saudi Arabia from the maps of other countries you have studied? What is the topography of the kingdom? What countries occupy its borders? What bodies of water?
- Click on **Geography** and then **Climate.** How does the climate of Saudi Arabia differ from that of other countries? What challenges do people face living in areas with little or no rainfall?
- How is water processed in a desalination plant?

Web site: http://www.arab.net/saudi/tour/sa_redsea.html
- Why is the Red Sea important to the city of Jeddah?

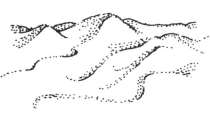

Web sites: http://www.wtgonline.com/country/sa/cli.html
http://www.infini.fr/~almegrji/climate.htm
- Click on **Climate.**
- What is the average yearly rainfall? What is the temperature range?
- When is the eastern part of the country bothered with sandstorms?
- What time of the year are temperatures most pleasant?
- Read the information and copy the map of the Arabian Peninsula. Label the cities.

Saudi Arabia
People

Web site: http://www.arab.net/saudi

- Click on **Culture** and then **People.** From what countries does most of the Saudi workforce come? Why would the immigrants want to live in Saudi Arabia? Why would Saudi Arabia depend upon foreign labor?
- What is the official **Religion** of the Kingdom of Saudi Arabia?

Web site: http://www.arab.net/saudi/culture/sa_clothing.html

- What is traditional dress for Saudi men and women? What is the reason for this manner of dress?
- What are the roles of mothers and fathers in the Saudi family structure? How are girls and boys raised differently?
- Search the Internet for pictures of traditional Saudi dress.

Saudi Arabia
Cities

Web site: http://www.arab.net/saudi/culture/saudi_culture.html

- Click on **Hajj.** Why do Muslims travel to Makkah each year? What is the significance of the Kaaba? What do the pilgrims do at Arafat? What services does the government offer the pilgrims?
- Write a diary explaining the activities of a typical Dhul Hijjah pilgrimage.
- Click on **Tents of the Arabian Desert.** How are Bedouin tents made? How are they furnished?

Web site: http://www.arab.net/saudi/tour/saudi_tour.html

- Select tour sites from the **central region,** the **eastern province,** the **southwest,** or the **western region.** In which region is the capital city? Where is Makkah?
- Which region includes the Asir National Park? Where was oil first discovered?
- Make a chart showing the attractions in each area.

Web site: http://www.arab.net/saudi/tour/sa_jeddahlife.html

- Read the information and click the camera icons to see photos of Jeddah. What leisure activities do the people enjoy?

Singapore

General Information

Web site: http://www.sg/

● Read the **History of Singapore** and click on the **Sir Stamford Raffles Page.**

✎ Design a picture postcard for some event in Singapore's history.

● Click on **One Minute Singapore** and then **People.** What ethnic groups live in Singapore? What is the major religion? What are the most popular **leisure** activities?

Web site: http://sunsite.nus.sg/SEAlinks/Singapore-photo.html

● Look at the picture of **public housing.** Why do you think most people in Singapore live in high-rise apartments?

Web site: http://sunsite.nus.sg/SEAlinks/singapore-info.html

● Use **Sunsite Singapore** for information about Southeast Asia. What other countries have you studied in this area? Where are they in relation to Singapore?

Search words:
Southeast Asia,
Malaysia

Singapore

Geography

Web site: http://www.odci.gov/cia/publications/nsolo/factbook/sn.htm

● What is the **climate** of Singapore? Name its **natural resources.** Why are **environmental issues** especially important in such a small country?

Web site: http://www.sg/

● Read the **History of Singapore** and click on the **nineteenth-century prints.**

✎ Design a travel brochure showing the topography of Singapore.

● Click on **One Minute Singapore** and read the information about **land and climate.** What are the geographical coordinates of Singapore? Print the map.

Web sites: http://sunsite.nus.sg/SEAlinks/maps/singapore.gif
http://sunsite.nus.sg/SEAlinks/maps/cia-SouthEastAsia.jpg

● Name three cities that are about five-hundred miles from the island of Singapore. How would you travel to them? Why do you think few people in Singapore have automobiles?

Singapore
Travel and Tourism

Web site: http://www.lonelyplanet.com/dest/sea/sing.htm

● View the **Slide Show.** How would you describe the city?
● What kinds of ethnic foods are available in Singapore? What is *nonya?*
● What are the prices for an average meal and hotel room?
● What might you see (and possibly buy) in Chinatown and Little India?
✎ If you traveled to Singapore, what other country(ies) might you wish to visit? Plan a two-week vacation in Southeast Asia. Visit at least three cities.
✎ Which would be a better job, ferryboat or rickshaw driver?

Web site: http://www.bus.orst.edu/faculty/larson/ba352/singaporeg1bad/project4.htm

● Read the information about **littering.** What do you think of the law regarding chewing gum? smoking?
✎ How do these restrictions affect tourists?

Singapore
Fine Arts

Web site: http://www.sac.com.sg/

● When will Singapore's new **Performing Arts Centre** open?
● What **theatres and facilities** will be included in the Esplanade?
● Click on **Art Links** and search the **Pan Shou Gallery.** Read about his life and work.
● Visit the **Lin Hsin Hsin Art** Museum. Use the **Museum Map** to experience Singaporean modern art and humor.

Web site: http://www.sg/infomap/martc/sso/

● Meet the Singapore Symphony Orchestra and read its history. In what European countries has the orchestra performed? Who is **Lan Shui?**

Web site: http://www.museum.org.sg/nhb.html

● From this site you can visit all the **national museums** of Singapore. Visit the **Civilisations Museum** to learn about various Asian cultures. You will see traditional crafts, sculpture, calligraphy, and artifacts.

South Africa

General Information

Web site: http://www.odci.gov/cia/publications/nsolo/factbook/sf.htm

- Draw the flag of South Africa.
- What are South Africa's natural resources?
- Who is the president of the country?
- Design an atlas page with names and pictures of South Africa's national symbols. Include a small map, a flag, and a summary of information about the country since 1994.
- What races of **people** make up the population of South Africa?
- Go to **Economy.** What are South Africa's industries? agricultural products?
- Choose one province or city to research further. Work with a group to organize a book about the regions or cities of South Africa. Print photos to illustrate your report.

Search words:
apartheid, Nelson Mandela, Mauritius, Swaziland, Lesotho

South Africa

Nature

Web site: http://africa.com/~venture/saparks/npbhome.htm

- Click on **Kruger National Park.** What wild animals roam freely in this game reserve? How are they protected? Which of the animals have you seen in a zoo?
- Is it possible to go on safari in South Africa? Search the Internet to learn what tourists do on a safari.

Web site: http://www.nbi.co.za/index.htm

- Click on **Botanical Gardens.** What is the most famous garden? Which garden is near Kruger National Park?
- Make a chart showing what a tourist can see and experience at the eight botanical gardens. Include details, such as varieties of plants, birds, animals, and outdoor activities.

South Africa

Cities

Web site: http://www.city.net/countries/south_africa/pretoria/
- What government buildings are located in Pretoria?
- What is a *jacaranda?* Why is Pretoria called the Jacaranda City?

Web site: http://www.city.net/countries/south_africa/johannesburg/
- How many official **languages** are recognized in South Africa?
- Click on **Fodor's Travel Tips** and find out what you should pack for a trip to Johannesburg. What should you plan to buy on a **shopping trip?**

Web site: http://www.city.net/countries/south_africa/cape_town/
- Select **Open World City Guide** and then **Getting Around Town.** What is the best way for a tourist to travel around Cape Town?
- Click on **Images of Cape Town.** What natural attraction is west of the city?
- Enlarge the sections of the **city center map** and join them. Locate a hotel in each corner of the city.

South Africa

Geography

Web site: http://www.lib.utexas.edu/Libs/PCL/Map_collection/africa/South_Africa.jpg
- Select **Geography.** Print the map.
- About how many miles would you travel between Cape Town and Bloemfontein? Bloemfontein and Johannesburg? Johannesburg and Pretoria?
- Draw a map of modern South Africa. Label the nine provinces, the kingdoms of Swaziland and Lesotho, and the capitals of Pretoria, Johannesburg, Cape Town, and Bloemfontein.

Web site: http://rapidtp.com/travel/centres.html
- Read about the natural beauty along the **Garden Route.** What could a tourist enjoy in the area? What is the climate?
- In what province is Pretoria?
- What is Gold Reef City?

Web site: http://www.city.net/countries/south_africa/
- What is the **weather today** in South Africa's major cities?
- Show the high and low temperatures on a bar graph and indicate the weather conditions with symbols.

Spain

General Information

Web site: http://www.red2000.com/spain/p-map.html

- Use this site for a photo tour of Spain. Enlarge the images for a better view.

Web site: http://www.city.net/countries/spain

- Click on **Spanish for Travellers.** Select a category of phrases, read the words, and listen to the pronunciations.
- In what countries is Spanish the official language?
- What is **today's weather** in the major cities of Spain?
- Click on **World Factbook;** go to **government.** When is Spain's independence day? Who is the chief of state?
- Go to **economy.** What are the chief industries and agricultural products of Spain?
- ✎ Show the high and low temperatures on a bar graph and indicate the weather conditions with symbols.

Search words:
Canary Islands, Iberia, Balearic Islands, Portugal

Spain

Geography

Web site: http://www.lib.utex.edu/Libs/PCL/Map_collection/europe/Spain.jpg

- Locate Madrid on the map and follow the road south to Cádiz. Name four cities you would pass along the way. What body of water must you cross to get to Tangier, Morocco? On what continent would your journey end?
- ✎ Use this information to design a topographical map of Spain. Include the Pyrenees Mountains, Meseta Central, and Cordillero Cantanbrica, as well as the Canary and Balearic Islands, bordering countries, and bodies of water.

Web sites: http://www.ececs.uc.edu/~sanfermin/TheBasques.html
http://www.techheadnet.com/ptexidor/catalan.htm

- Use the information to make a population map. Mark the regions where each group lives and create a chart of ethnic characteristics.
- Read about the Basques and the Catalans, two distinct ethnic groups of Spain.

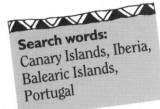

Spain

Culture and Customs

Web sites: http://www.red2000.com/spain/toros/index.html
http://www.cyberspain.com/life/toros.htm

● These sites offer historical information about bullfighting. Read about a Corrida.

✎ Use bullfighting terms to make a Spanish dictionary.

Web sites: http://www.red2000.com/spain/flamenco/index.html
http://www.cyberspain.com/life/flamenco.htm

● Read the background of the art of **Flamenco.** Use the links to view images of Flamenco performers.

Web site: http://www.docuweb.ca/SiSpain/english/travelli/

● Read about Spain's **social customs.** Why do many Spanish businesses observe an afternoon siesta?

Web site: http://www.red2000.com/spain/f-map.html

● Use the clickable map to choose a location. Read about local fiestas and folklore.

✎ Choose one city and create a poster or calendar about local customs that would attract tourists.

Spain

Cities and Landmarks

Web site: http://www.red2000.com/spain/primer/arch.html

● Learn about the styles of Spain's finest **architecture.** Click on the icons for a view of the **Great Mosque,** the **Alhambra,** and the Church of the **Sagrada Familia.** How is the Spanish style unique?

Web sites: http://www.red2000.com/spain/t-map.html
http://www.cyberspain.com/

● Select a city from the map and read about its tourist attractions. See each major city of Spain through a photo tour and sightseeing guide plus plenty of clickable camera icons.

✎ Plan menus of local cuisine from the gastronomy links.

✎ Work with a group to create a sightseeing map of Spain. Include printed photos and label the landmarks.

Web site: http://www.spaintour.es/

● Click on **sun and beaches.** Locate the four beaches on a map. Click on **Tourist Info** for addresses of information offices around the country.

✎ Choose a city and write for tourist brochures.

Sweden

General Information

Web site: http://www.lib.utex.edu/Libs/PCL/Map_collection/europe/Sweden.ipg
- Study the map of Sweden. How could you travel from one end of the country to the other? Locate Stockholm. About how many miles is Stockholm from Helsinki, Finland?

Web site: http://www.visiteurope.com/Sweden/Sweden01.htm
- What is the capital city of Sweden? What are the three largest cities? What is the population of the entire country?

Web site: http://www.gosweden.org/
- Read the **Heritage and History** of Sweden. When did the first people come to live in the area? What effect did the Vikings have on the region?
- Describe Sweden's natural beauty. Why is Sweden a good place to live?
- How many Swedes have emigrated to the United States? Where did they settle? What is Sweden's relationship with the United States today?

Search words:
Vikings, archipelago, Lapland

Sweden

Stockholm

Web site: http://www.stoinfo.se/england/
- Click on **Archipelago.** What is an archipelago? Why are the towns of Grinda and Sandhamn important? How can they be reached?

Web site: http://www.smorgasbord.se/sweden/natrecspo/nature/every.html
- What is *Allemansratten*? Explain what a person may or may not do.
- Do you think a practice like Allemansratten would work in the United States? Explain.

Web site: http://www.smorgasbord.se//provincial/stockholm/
- Click on **Useful Information** and read how to book a sightseeing tour or make a telephone call.

Sweden

Culture and Tradition

Web site: http://www.gosweden.org/seasongate.html

● Read Swedish **traditions** for each season of the year.

✎ Design a calendar with picture symbols of Sweden's traditions.

Web site: http://www.gosweden.org/culture.html

● Why are Sweden's artistic traditions distinctive?

● Who was Alfred Nobel? What did he invent? Use the link to visit the official web site of the Nobel Foundation.

✎ In what professions are Nobel Prizes awarded? Search the Internet for information about one former Nobel Prize winner.

Web site: http://www.stockholm98.se

● Stockholm has been designated the Cultural Capital of Europe in 1998 by the European Union. How will the city be transformed for the events? What is the **program?**

● What will be the **seven high points** of the celebration? Which event would you most like to attend? Explain.

Sweden

Travel and Tourism

Web site: http://www.swedenguide.com

● Click on The Country of Sweden. Why is Sweden called the land of sunlit summer nights? What other world cities lie on the 60th parallel of latitude?

✎ How might tourists be affected visiting a city where the sun never sets?

Web site: http://www.tourist-offices.org.uk/Sweden/Sweden.html

● Go to **Travel Facts.** Read about the effects of the midnight sun on the lives of the Swedish people.

Web site: http://www.travelfile.com/go/SWEDEN.html

● Click on **Adventures** and **Ice Hotel.** Describe the world's largest igloo. Where is it located and when is it open each year? Would you enjoy this kind of vacation? Explain.

✎ Click on **National Parks.** Label a country map with the names of Sweden's parks. Include the date when each park was founded.

Web site: http://www.smorgasbord.se//provincial/

● Select any of the **provinces** to learn what to see and do outside the major cities. Look carefully at the images. How do the location and geography of the area affect daily life and leisure activities?

Switzerland

General Information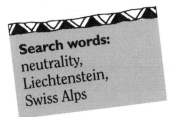

Web site: http://www.lib.utex.edu/Libs/PCL/Map_collection/europe/Switzerland.jpg

● Describe the locations of Berne, Lucerne, Geneva, and Zurich. Which of these cities is not situated on a lake?

Web site: http://www.ethz.ch/swiss/Switzerland_Hist_Details.html

✎ Use the time line of history to create an illustrated time line of five important events.

Web site: http://www.swissinfo.ch/swissinfo/general/swiss.htm

● Study the **Language map** of Switzerland. What languages are spoken? Which is the most common? least common?

Search words:
neutrality,
Liechtenstein,
Swiss Alps

Switzerland

Geography

Web site: http://www.swissinfo.ch/swissinfo/general/swiss.htm

● Read **Switzerland is situated in the heart of Europe.** Look at the map showing the topography of the country. Which region is the largest?
● Read **The Swiss work within narrow confines.** In which physical region do most of the people live? Discuss the density of population.
● Read **Steppeland grasses grow in Switzerland.** How do the mountains affect the climate and weather conditions?

Web site: http://www.ethz.ch/swiss/Switzerland_Info.html

● What countries border Switzerland?
● What is a *canton*? How many are there in Switzerland?
● Click on **more information** to read details about Switzerland's geography. Which canton has the most mountains? the most glaciers?
● Use the chart to estimate driving times between major cities.
✎ Create a map indicating cities and drive times.

Switzerland

Winter Sports

Web site: http://www.swissinfo.ch/swissinfo/general/ski.htm
- Look at the photos of Swiss winter sports.
- ✎ What conditions and equipment are necessary for each of these sports? Where else in the world can these sports be enjoyed?

Web site: http://copper.ucs.indiana.edu/~wamyers/zwww/swisst/swiss.html
- Look at photos of a hike through the Swiss Alps. What problems and pleasures might the Swiss experience in living in the Alps?

Web sites: http://www.actionsites.com/skiing/swizerma.htm
http://worldserver.com/ski/switzerland/zermatt/zermatte.html
- Read about **Zermatt,** one of the world's finest ski resorts.
  Describe the facilities for skiers. What could you do if you did not want to ski?
- ✎ You may request a brochure and then design a brochure of your own illustrating Zermatt's features.

Web site: http://www.davos.ch/topic_e.html
- Check the Live Cam for a weather and snow report.

Switzerland

Travel and Tourism

Web site: http://www.travelchannel.com/spot/lucerne/welcome.htm
- What **attractions** are available for tourists in Lucerne?

Web site: http://www.zurich.ch/
- Click on **Pictures** to see images of Zurich.
- ✎ Compare a visit to Lucerne with one to Zurich.

Web site: http://rtk.ch/alehamann/Gallery_Swiss_mountains.html
- ✎ You can enlarge these photos of Switzerland's most beautiful mountains.
- ✎ Search the Internet for the heights of two mountains of your choosing.

Taiwan

General Information

Web site: http://www.leksu.com/faq.html

- Check **Frequently Asked Questions** to identify the four ethnic groups of Taiwan. What are the characteristics of each group? Where do they live? How do they earn a living?
- What is the total **population?** In which part of the island do most of the people live?

Web site: http://www.odci.gov/cia/publications/nsolo/factbook/tw.htm

- Go to **People.** What is the official language? What is the life expectancy for men? women?
- Go to **Economy.** What are the chief agricultural and industrial products? Who are Taiwan's chief trading partners?

Web site: http://www.gio.gov.tw/info/ecology/cover.html

- Click on **environment.** What wildlife is native to the island?
  What is the government doing to conserve and protect the animals?
- ✎ Make a chart (or book) indicating the description, diet, and habitat of **Taiwan's Endemic Wildlife.** Include illustrations and explain if each animal is endangered or threatened.

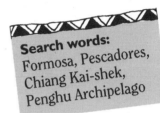

Search words:
Formosa, Pescadores,
Chiang Kai-shek,
Penghu Archipelago

Taiwan

Geography

Web site: http://www.leksu.com/faq.html

- Check the **Frequently Asked Questions** to learn the location of Taiwan. How do geologists believe the island was formed?
- Read about the **topography and natural resources** of Taiwan. What are the island's natural resources?
- How much of the island is covered with mountains? What is the highest peak?

Web site: http://www.softidea.com/twhakkausa/taiwan_info.html

- Where is Taiwan located in relation to mainland China? How many miles is it from Shanghai? Hong Kong?
- What are the major cities on the island?
- What are the chief crops of Taiwan?

Web site: http://www.wtgonline.com/country/tw/cli.html

- Read the summary information about Taiwan's climate.
- Click on **Climate Chart Page.** What was the average humidity level in Taipei? Which three months had the highest rainfall?

Taiwan
Culture

Web site: http://www.gio.gov.tw/info/culture/culture.html

● This complete government site covers the culture of Taiwan. Click on the image for information.

✎ Choose one of the thirty areas of culture to write about in depth. Make drawings to illustrate your report.

✎ Organize the links in alphabetical order and create a culture dictionary.

Web site: http://www.geocities.com/Tokyo/7031/culture.htm

● How do the Taiwanese celebrate the Chinese New Year? Read about the other festivals. List them in order by month.

✎ Design a postcard for one festival and send it with a message to one of your friends.

● What examples of **Chinese Folk Art** are made in Taiwan?

Taiwan
Attractions

Web site: http://www.geocities.com/Tokyo/7031/taiwansights.htm

● This site presents photos and descriptions of the natural beauty of Taiwan. What can a visitor to the Northern Coast National Scenic Area see and do?

Web site: http://www.asiaway.com/tai/trav.htm

✎ Click on sites for several of Taiwan's attractions. Which ones are natural, and which are human-made? Which have some connection to religion? Make a chart to show the three categories.

● Go to **Southern Taiwan 2** and read about the Penghu Islands in **Islands Apart.** How would a visit to the Penghu Islands beach be different from the **Tropical Beaches** of Taiwan?

Web site: http://www.npm.gov.tw/

● View the collection of Chinese art and calligraphy at the National Palace Museum. What differences do you notice between European and Asian art?

Thailand

General Information

Web site: http://www.siam.net/guide/html/general.html

- Read the **General Information** about Thailand. What is the meaning of the word *Thailand?*
- What are the official **language** and most common **religion?**
- Go to **Things To Know.** What is the population of the country? What is the capital city?
- When is the King's Birthday? the Queen's Birthday?
- Go to **Sports.** What two unusual sports are popular in Thailand?
- ✎ In what other country do people practice kite fighting? Look for images on the Internet and design an Asian-style kite.

Web site: http://www.odci.gov/cia/publications/nsolo/factbook/th.htm

- With what countries does Thailand have **border disputes?**
- What are Thailand's natural resources?
- What **environmental hazards** threaten Thailand's environment and wildlife?
- What type of **government** does Thailand have? Who is the chief of state?
- Who is the U.S. ambassador to Thailand?

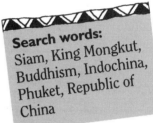

Search words:
Siam, King Mongkut, Buddhism, Indochina, Phuket, Republic of China

Thailand

Geography

Web site: http://www.cs.ait.ac.th/~wutt/prehi.html

- Read information about Thailand's **Prehistory.** What artifacts have archaeologists uncovered? Who were the Ban Chiang people? Trace their migration to Thailand.

Web site: http://www.siam.net/guide/html/general.html

- What is the **climate** of Thailand? What causes the summer monsoons? What is the best time of year to visit Thailand?
- From what countries have immigrants come to live in Thailand?

Web site: http://www.snamcn.su.ac.th/thailand/geography/geography.htm

- Where is Thailand? What are its neighboring countries?
- What European country is about the same size as Thailand?

Web site: http://www.phuket.com/island/info.htm

- Where is Phuket Island? Of what is it made? Who lives there? What are its main industries?

Thailand
Customs and Tradition

Web site: http://www.siam.net/guide/html/general.html
● Read about the **Local Customs.** What do Thais believe about the head and feet? What is the traditional Thai greeting?

Web site: http://www.sino.net/asean/thailand.html
● Go to **People and Culture.** What is the influence of Thai women in the home? in public?

Web site: http://www.tat.or.th/general/dodont.html
● How do the Thai people honor their king at the cinema?
● What rules must be observed when visiting a Buddhist temple?
● What honor is paid the Buddhist monks?
● Explain the Thai custom for addressing people by their first name.

Thailand
Attractions and Landmarks

Web site: http://www.asiatour.com/thailand/
● Select **d-03bang,** and then **dt-ba378,** from the directories.
● Click on the **Grand Palace.** Study the map. Where is the entrance? Coin Pavilion? Boromphiman Hall?
● What is proper dress for visiting the palace compound?
● What is inside the **Wat Phra Kaeo?** Be sure to view the other Buddhist temples.

Web site: http://www.siam.net/guide/index.html
● Click on **Bangkok** and read about the founding of the city.
View the **Pictures** to see the sights. How many of the monuments have a connection to Buddhism?
● What items are good values for shoppers?
✎ Select another city to visit. Look at the **Pictures.** How would you describe the topography of the location? What kinds of activities are possible? Design a travel poster for your city.
✎ How important is natural beauty and location to the tourist business of Thailand? Explain.

Turkey

General Information

Web site: http://www.odci.gov/cia/publications/nsolo/factbook/tu.htm

- What are the **geographic coordinates** of Turkey? What bodies of water border the country? What countries border Turkey?
- What is Turkey's main **religion?**
- What is the **climate** and **terrain** of the country?
- What are Turkey's natural resources?
- Go to **Economy.** What are the main agricultural and industrial products? What commodities are exported? Is the U.S. an important trade partner with Turkey?
- ✎ Look around a shopping district near you for a Turkish import. Report your findings to the class.

Web site: http://www.turkey.org/tourism.htm

- Choose three **cities** or **regions** to explore. Read the information and describe the tourist attractions in the area. Be sure to summarize the city's history.
- ✎ Write postcards from three cities.

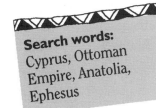

Search words:
Cyprus, Ottoman Empire, Anatolia, Ephesus

Turkey

Culture and Cuisine

Web sites: http://www.turkey.org/c_dance.htm
http://www.mfa.gov.tr/GRUPD/culture.htm

- Read about the different styles of Turkish folk dance. Who are the performers? What occasions call for a dance?
- Listen to samples of Turkish folk music.

Web sites: http://www.turkey.org/c_carpet.htm
http://www.mfa.gov.tr/GRUPD/culture.htm

- From what fibers are the carpets made? What is a *kilim?* How are carpets used in mosques throughout the country?

Web site: http://www.turkey.org/c_coffee.htm

- When was coffee brought to Istanbul? How is it different from coffee served in America?

Web sites: http://www.turkey.org/c_cuisin.htm
http://www.mfa.gov.tr/GRUPD/culture.htm

- What dishes are unique to Turkish cuisine?
- ✎ Which Turkish foods have you eaten? Which would you be willing to sample?

Turkey
Istanbul

Web sites: http://www.turkey.org/tourism.htm
http://www.duke.edu/~emin/ISTANBUL/PLACES/ayasofya.html

- Read the information about **Istanbul** and then click on **museums** and go to the Aya Sofya (Haghia Sophia). Explain the history and present condition of the mosque. What is on display there?
- Visit the bazaars of Istanbul. What products are available there? How does shopping differ in America?
- Make a list of five items you might purchase in a Turkish bazaar. Search the tourism site to find the name of Turkish money.

Web site: http://www.city.net/countries/turkey/istanbul/

- Click on **Maps.** Where is Istanbul located? Why do you think this location is a good one?
- What is the **Istanbul Bogazi?** Why is it popular with tourists?
- Look at **Istanbul in Pictures.** What can you learn about the city from the aerial photos?
- What will the **weather** conditions be for the next five days? What are the best months to visit Turkey?

Turkey
Geography

Web site: http://www.turknet.com/turkey/landscape/natural.html

- Explain the diversity of the Turkish landscape. What popular spring flower originated in Turkey?
- What fruits and nuts originated in Turkey?
- Have you ever eaten food imported from Turkey? If so, what have you eaten and how was it prepared? If possible, share a snack of dried apricots and almonds with the class.

Web site: http://yarra.vicnet.net.au/~focus/c_ana_mn.htm

- Click on **Ancient Civilizations and Cities** to view artifacts and read information about the ancient cities.
- Make drawings of six artifacts. Write a brief description of each and indicate the city where it was uncovered.

Ukraine

General Information

Web site: http://www.wtgonline.com/country/ua/gen.html
- What are the official language and religion of Ukraine?
- Click on **Travel.** How long is a flight from Kiev to London? Moscow? Vienna? Trace the routes on a map.
- Click on **Essentials.** What precautions must a traveler remember about **food and drink?** What diseases may be a problem?

Web site: http://www.odci.gov/cia/publications/nsolo/factbook/up.htm
- What is the **population** of Ukraine? What is the **life expectancy** of males? females?
- Go to **Economy.** What is Ukraine's national **currency** called? What products does it export?
- Go to **Government.** When did Ukraine become independent from the Soviet Union? Who is the current chief of state?

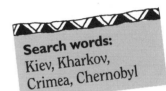

Search words:
Kiev, Kharkov, Crimea, Chernobyl

Web site: http://www.cs.unc.edu/~yakowenk/pysanky.html
- This site has wonderful images and directions for making *pysanky* (Ukranian Easter eggs).
- ✎ If possible, try dying some eggs. You may prefer to draw several of the symbols, giving each an appropriate color and explaining its meaning.

Ukraine

Geography

Web site: http://www.undp.org/missions/ukraine/
- Click on **Map** and **Facts and Figures.** What countries border Ukraine? Give the compass direction from Ukraine to each border country.
- About how many miles is it across Ukraine, north to south? west to east?

Web site: http://www.undp.org/missions/ukraine/
- Click on **Facts and Figures.** What mountains occupy the west? the south?
- What is the **climate?** Which area would a tourist be most likely to visit? Explain what they would see and do there.
- ✎ Draw a map showing Ukraine's major cities, mountains, border countries, and bodies of water.

Web site: http://www.brama.com/travel/index.html
- Use this site to determine **distances** between Ukrainian cities. Choose six cities, mark the routes between them, and indicate the distances by reading the charts.

United Kingdom

General Information

Web site: http://www.wtgonline.com/country/uk/gen.html

- What countries make up the United Kingdom? Click on the links. What are the capitals? populations? languages?
- Name the three Channel Islands. Click on the links. Which one has the largest area? population? Describe the geographic location of each island.
- Click on **Map Page.** Where is the United Kingdom located in Europe? You may enlarge the maps by clicking on the country names.
- Go to **Government.** Who leads Parliament? Name the political parties. How often are elections held?
- Click on **Climate.** What is the weather like in the United Kingdom?

Web site: http://www.odci.gov/cia/publications/nsolo/factbook/uk.htm

- Go to **Geography** and then **International Disputes.** Read the information and locate the disputed areas on a map.
- What are the **highest** and **lowest points** in the United Kingdom?
- Go to **People.** Which population group is the largest?
- Go to **Economy.** What does the United Kingdom export? import?

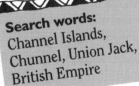

Search words:
Channel Islands,
Chunnel, Union Jack,
British Empire

United Kingdom

Attractions and Landmarks

Web site: http://www.voicenet.com/~dravyk/toltour/

- Take the **Virtual Tour** of the Tower of London. What might a visitor see in the Jewel House? the Royal Armourie? What famous prisoners were held at the tower? Who are the Yeoman Warders?

Web sites: http://www.uk-guide.com/london/buckpala.htm
http://www.royal.gov.uk/palaces/index.htm

- Read about **Buckingham Palace, State Rooms, Royal Mews,** and **Queen's Gallery.**

Web site: http://www.openworld.co.uk/britain/

- You can access attractions in **Bath, York, Chester, Edinburgh,** and **London** from this site. Click on links for information and images.
- ✎ Work with a group. Each student should select a city, search the information, and print the images. Combine all the cities in a class reference book.

Web site: http://www.activemind.com/Mysterious/Topics/Stonehenge

- Learn the story of Stonehenge and locate it on a map. Visit the **Picture Gallery** and several **links.**
- ✎ Considering all the information, who do you think built Stonehenge?

United Kingdom

London

Web site: http://www.cineworld.com/Main/main_screen.html

- Click on **London** for information and **sightseeing movies** on Westminster Abbey, Trafalgar Square, Tower of London, and Parliament.
- Click on **Cultural Information** to learn the schedule for the changing of the guard at Buckingham Palace.
- Print a **walking map** for a trip that includes Westminster Abbey and Parliament. Trace the path.

Web site: http://www.uktravel.com/london.html

- Use the **London Active Map** to locate attractions on the railroad or underground. Locate **Covent Garden.** What can a tourist do there?
- Which direction would you travel from **St. Paul's** to **Hyde Park Corner?** from **Oxford Circus** to **Knightsbridge?**
- Search the Internet for additional information about Harrod's.
- What attractions surround **Charing Cross** and **Westminster** stations?

United Kingdom

Famous People

Web site: http://www.winstonchurchill.org/

- This site offers a **photo** history of the life of Britain's most famous prime minister. Describe his physical appearance. When did Churchill lead Great Britain?

Web site: http://www.cs.strath.ac.uk/Contrib/JMC/

- Who was **John Muir?** Where was he born? What were his contributions to the environment and the U.S. park system?
- Research information about the **Sierra Club.** What are its current environmental concerns?

Web sites: http://www.palomar.edu/Library/shake.htm
http://www.rdg.ac.uk/globe/

- Read a short biography of William Shakespeare. Where was he born? What did he do?
- Click on **Five Diamond Sites.** Take the **virtual tour** of the new **Globe Theatre.** What happened to the first Globe?
- Make a list of ten works by Shakespeare.

Web site: http://www.royal.gov.uk/family/index.htm

- These pages contain biographies and photos of the members of Britain's **Royal Family.**

United Kingdom
Scotland

Web site: http://www.uktravel.com/uk/scotland.html
- From this site you can find information about six of Scotland's towns and cities. Choose one to read and report on.
- From the **Edinburgh** site you can find a **map of the city centre** with links to all the major attractions in the capital.

Web sites: http://www.royal.gov.uk/palaces/holyrood.htm
http://lynn.efr.hw.ac.uk/EDC/guide/holyrood.html
- When and by whom is the Palace of Holyroodhouse used?
- Retell the story of Mary Queen of Scots.

Web site: http://alpha.wcoil.com/~highlndr/main.html
- This page has lots of links for things to do and see in Scotland. Read a history of the **kilt** and listen to the music of a **bagpipe.**
- Visit **Clans on the Web.** Make a list of ten Scottish last names. Choose a **tartan** to copy.
- Read the **Legend** of Nessie and visit three related sites. Locate Loch Ness on a map.
- What is **haggis?** How is it prepared? Would you be willing to try haggis if you were visiting Scotland?

United Kingdom
Wales

Web site: http://www.data-wales.co.uk/index.htm
- Click on the **Data Wales Maps Page.** Go to the **Main Roads** map. List four cities along A470. Which direction does it run through the country? Where is the airport? Highway A5?
- Click on **Language, Currency, National Symbols, etc.** Describe the flag of Wales. Why is the leek the emblem of Wales?

Web site: http://www.castlewales.com/home.html
- This site has high-quality photos and information about 170 castles in Wales. Go to **different types of castles** and **The Age of the Castle.** Into what three main categories are the castles divided?
- Make a dictionary of castle terms: *keep, bailey, battlement, moat,* and so on.

Web site: http://arachnid.cs.cf.ac.uk/Guide/wales
- This site has links to Wales's six geographic counties.
- Go to **Cardiff,** the capital city. What are the main attractions?
- Draw a map of Wales, marking the counties and capital city.

Zimbabwe

General Information

Web site: http://www.odci.gov/cia/publications/nsolo/factbook/zi.htm

● Go to **People.** What is the life expectancy of men and women in Zimbabwe? What is the **official language?**

● What is the **capital** city? When is Zimbabwe's **Independence** Day? What was Zimbabwe called before its independence?

Web site: http://www.mediazw.com/index.html

● Choose **Things to do, places to see,** then **National Parks.** Read about the **Safari Areas.** How are the areas used besides for sport hunting? Read the information on six areas.

✎ Make a chart showing the size of each area, its terrain, and how it is used. What are the pros and cons of the safari business?

Web site: http://www.mother.com/~zimweb/Dzimbabwe.html

● Use the clickable **flag** to learn the meaning of its colors.

✎ Draw a flag and label the bars.

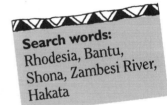

Search words:
Rhodesia, Bantu,
Shona, Zambesi River,
Hakata

Zimbabwe

Geography

Web sites: http://www.odci.gov/cia/publications/nsolo/factbook/zi.htm
http://www.africanet.com/africanet/country/zimbabwe/default.htm

● Where is Zimbabwe? What is its total **land area?** Describe its **terrain** and **climate.**

● What are the major towns? Where is the capital?

● What countries border Zimbabwe? What rivers flow along the borders?

✎ What environmental issues does Zimbabwe face? How do those issues affect the quality of life in the country?

Web sites: http://www.africaonline.com/AfricaOnline/travel/zimbabwe/attractions.html
http://cy.co.za/atg/stbroz.html

● Why do tourists visit **Victoria Falls? Great Zimbabwe?**
What wildlife lives in the **Mana Pools** National Park during the dry season?

✎ Search the Internet to learn about efforts to save the black rhino from extinction.

Web site: http://www.africanet.com/africanet/country/zimbabwe/default.htm

● Click on **Economy.** What agricultural products are grown in Zimbabwe? Go to **Climate.** How does the climate affect growing conditions?

Glossary

Bookmarks: A feature that saves and organizes URLs so that you can find them quickly at a later time (sometimes called Favorites).

Browser: A term that identifies the kinds of software you use to access the html pages.

Electronic Mail (E-Mail): A means of sending messages from one Internet user to another.

Frequently Asked Questions (FAQs): Text containing answers to questions commonly asked about a specific topic.

Gopher: A text-only information system.

Graphics Interchange Format (GIF): An image file format.

Home Page: The opening page of a Web site. It contains links to additional and related information.

Hypertext: The words on the screen that are a different color from the rest. They may be underlined. If you place the cursor on these words or phrases, a pointed finger will appear. Click the mouse and download an image, sound, or another Web page.

Hypertext Markup Language (HTML): Language used to create Web pages.

Hypertext Transfer Protocol (HTTP): The way your Web browser speaks to the Web server program on the World Wide Web.

Icon: A small picture or symbol that represents something. Point your cursor at the icon, click, and start the application.

Internet: A matrix of networks that connects computers around the world.

Modem: Equipment that connects a computer to a telephone line.

Mouse: A small device that connects to the computer and directs the movement of the cursor around the screen.

Online: Connected to the Internet, either sending or receiving information.

Search Engine: A program that uses key words to search all Web pages and sort out sites having the information you have requested.

Uniform Resource Locator (URL): The address of a Web site.

Web Site: The location on the World Wide Web where you can find specific information.